Estate Planning for Everyone

Estate Planning
The whole truth—

Patrick F. Flaherty
and Richard S. Ziegler

for Everyone

Revised
Edition

from planning to probate

HARPER & ROW, PUBLISHERS
Cambridge, Hagerstown, Philadelphia, San Francisco,
London, Mexico City, São Paulo, Sydney

1817

Clearfield

ESTATE PLANNING FOR EVERYONE *Revised Edition*. Copyright © 1981 by Patrick F. Flaherty and Richard S. Ziegler. All rights reserved. Printed in the United States of America. No part of this book may be used or reproduced in any manner whatsoever without written permission except in the case of brief quotations embodied in critical articles and reviews. For information address Harper & Row, Publishers, Inc., 10 East 53rd Street, New York, N.Y. 10022. Published simultaneously in Canada by Fitzhenry & Whiteside Limited, Toronto.

Designer: Ruth Bornschlegel

Library of Congress Cataloging in Publication Data

Flaherty, Patrick F
  Estate planning for everyone.

  Includes index.
  1. Estate planning—United States—Popular works.
I. Ziegler, Richard S., joint author. II. Title.
KF750.Z9Z5 1981   346.7305'2   80-8314
ISBN 0-690-01943-2

81 82 83 84 85 10 9 8 7 6 5 4 3 2 1

Contents

Authors' note

This is the decade of the '80s. Inflation seems to have become a way of life. Attitudes are changing. Goals are changing. Investments are changing. Values are changing. But one thing has not changed—the need to keep your estate plan up to date. In fact, now more than ever, thinking people want to do everything they can to make sure their affairs are in proper order.

This is the revised edition of *Estate Planning for Everyone.* We have expanded several sections to provide more specific counsel, have updated the sample estate plans, and included information to show you how to take advantage of the sweeping changes resulting from the 1976 Tax Reform Act and the Revenue Act of 1978. This legislation makes it essential for you to review your personal and your family's estate planning. Failure to do so may result in your paying higher taxes while you live and your heirs doing so after you die.

Our book is designed as a guide to help you plan your estate to achieve long-term goals, to save on taxes, and to assure greater protection of assets for family security and well-being. It explains legal terms and concepts in a way that is easy to read and understand. It takes the mystery out of estate planning.

The text reflects our personal experiences as estate planning attorneys. Some details of our advice may vary in different states, but the principles are applicable across the country. In the pages that follow, you will learn why we believe that a properly planned estate is one of the best gifts any man or woman can leave his or her heirs.

Patrick F. Flaherty and Richard S. Ziegler

Estate Planning for Everyone

1

Your estate

- **HOW PROPERTY IS HELD**
- **WHAT HAPPENS TO IT WHEN YOU DIE**

Estate planning is one of the most important responsibilities an individual has. It is the development of a plan to manage and dispose of the assets and liabilities you leave at death in a way best suited to the needs of your beneficiaries.

Most estates involve a home, savings, investments, life insurance, and personal belongings. Wise estate planning can enable you, your family, and your other beneficiaries to retain a greater share of your estate by providing for its proper management and enjoyment and minimizing the erosion of taxes.

You are richer than you think. The average middle-class American owns a car, a home, and furnishings, and has some savings, life insurance, and pension benefits. Others may have investments in real estate, stocks and bonds, or an interest in a business such as a small corporation, partnership, or proprietorship. The value of many of these investments will fluctuate depending on supply and demand. Your hope, of course, is that they will increase in value and will also provide income. Over the years, the total estates of many families will grow to a sizable sum. Wise estate planning will not only help to boost the worth of your estate, but can also keep taxes at a more reasonable level.

Whatever the form of your wealth, you have silent partners: the federal government and, often, state and local authorities. They levy taxes on money when you receive it and when you leave it.

In recent years, two things have become major concerns for everyone who owns anything: inflation and taxes. Proper financial planning can be beneficial in dealing with both problems. There are limits to what one person can do about inflation, but there are many things you

1

can do about the costs and problems of transferring the things you own to your family and loved ones at your death.

This book discusses, in a general way, questions about wills, probate, taxes, legal fees, and many of the complications involved in death and inheritance. This information will not make you an estate planner or financial adviser, but it will make you aware of the problems and help you to understand the methods you can use to solve them and judge the competency of your advisers.

This is not a "do-it-yourself" book, because the business of estate planning is too important to be left to the untrained. You get no second chance to come back and correct your mistakes.

The single most important step in estate planning is to make a will. This last testament serves two basic purposes: to set down, in writing, how you wish your property to be distributed after your death and who you want to do the job.

When there's no will, your estate will be distributed according to the laws of the state in which you live, not as you may want. The lack of a will can be difficult for your heirs and lead to unforeseen results and unnecessary taxes and expenses.

WHAT IS PROPERTY?

The technical name for things that people acquire is *property.* This general term means anything capable of being owned: real estate, personal belongings, automobiles, clothing, household furnishings, savings, investments, and so on.

Specifically, property can be divided into two categories:

1. Real estate, which includes not only land but also buildings and other fixtures permanently attached to it.
2. Personal property, of which there are two types:
   a. *Tangible:* that which you can touch, such as a car, clothing, or a painting.
   b. *Intangible:* that which represents ownership, such as a stock certificate or savings account.

OWNERSHIP OF PROPERTY To own property means to possess or hold it and to enjoy or control its private use. There are several different ways in which owners hold their property. Each is treated differently at the owner's death.

The following are common ways of holding property:

1. In Your Own Name. Usually, we think of property as being held in an individual's own name. This is sometimes referred to as "sole-name" ownership. No one else has any interest in the property.

Often, sole-name ownership involves some kind of registration in which your name is actually associated with the property in a formal manner. If you buy a piece of real estate, you will receive a deed on which your name will appear as the owner. If the deed is recorded, the property rolls in the county in which the property is located will list your name as the owner, and a local unit of government will recognize this possession by levying taxes and sending you the bill.

Other kinds of investment property are also subject to sole-name ownership and formal registration. For example, the owner's name will be inserted on the certificate of shares of stock or registered bonds of a business corporation and will also be shown on the books and records of the company.

Some kinds of sole-name ownership do not involve formal registration, so that possession of such property becomes your only evidence of ownership. This is usually the case when you purchase a painting or receive a gift of cash.

2. Ownership with Others. Sometimes shared ownership may be necessary and desirable. Such situations occur when ownership involves property that cannot be divided without destroying its function. Examples are a piece of real estate that cannot be divided easily: for example, a homestead or property owned by two or more individuals who plan to use it in a business venture such as a partnership.

Often, shared ownership is subject to a written agreement, and in some cases is submitted to formal registration.

The two most common forms of ownership with others are *joint tenancy* and *tenancy in common.* Their effects are more complex and far reaching than you may realize. Here's what each term means:

JOINT TENANCY With this arrangement, two or more individuals own an undivided portion of the property's total value. If there are two joint tenants, each owns an undivided half; if three, each owns an undivided third; and so on. This type of ownership is the subject of a separate chapter.

In legal terms, "undivided portion" means that there is no identification of any joint tenant with any specific portion of the property. Each interest covers the whole. Each tenant owns a fraction of the entire value, usually in proportion to the original investment.

In the event of the death of one of the joint tenants, his or her entire interest in the property automatically goes to the surviving joint tenant or tenants. This is called *right of survivorship.* When we say *automatically,* we mean that this process of transfer takes place without reference to the deceased joint tenant's will or the probate of that will. The deceased joint tenant's will, if he or she has one, has absolutely *no effect* on the joint tenancy property. The reason why so many property owners use joint tenancy is to facilitate the transfer of property to a surviving joint tenant (most often a spouse or other family member) in the event of death without the necessity of probate. Joint tenancy must be created by a *writing* which mentions the right of survivorship.

TENANCY IN COMMON This is exactly like joint tenancy except that there is no right of survivorship or automatic transfer at death. If two persons own a piece of real estate as tenants in common, and one of them dies, the share of the property belonging to the deceased tenant in common passes by means of his or her will, or if there is no will, according to applicable state laws. Generally, each cotenant's share of the property is treated as though it were owned separately. For example, if spouses hold property as tenants in common, the survivor does not automatically receive the deceased spouse's share. The deceased spouse's share is subject to probate. The surviving spouse must depend on a will or state law establishing a spouse's share. These laws vary from state to state and the size of the share may depend on how many children also survive.

Here are some additional types of property ownership:

TENANCY BY THE ENTIRETIES is a particular kind of joint tenancy between spouses. It cannot be changed unless both spouses agree. Some states do not recognize this kind of holding.

PARTNERSHIP An oral or written understanding underlies this kind of ownership. Commonly, it's a combination of two or more individuals, each contributing property (money, real estate, or the like) and agreeing that it will be used in a certain manner, usually in a business venture.

Unless the partnership agreement provides otherwise, at the death of one owner the partnership will terminate and the deceased partner's share of the assets will be distributed in accordance with his will or applicable state laws in a probate proceeding.

To be in a partnership without a specific, written agreement is pure folly. Misunderstandings can arise when there are no clearly defined provisions. Even if you and your partners get along fine while you are alive, the lack of a written statement can cause problems at death.

In all partnerships, spell out the responsibilities of ownership, preferably with the aid of an attorney.

COMMUNITY PROPERTY In certain states, the laws provide that property acquired during marriage by means other than gift or inheritance is owned equally by husband and wife. With some exceptions, when one spouse dies, his or her estate consists of one half of these community property assets.

At present, community property states are Arizona, California, Idaho, Louisiana, Nevada, New Mexico, Texas, and Washington. Similar laws in Hawaii, Michigan, Nebraska, Oklahoma, and Oregon have been repealed.

The historical basis for community property ownership is found in Spanish, Mexican, and French law. It's a lot like having a marital partnership. By law, the man is the administrator, but both persons have the same interest in all property and in all income generated by either party's labor. At death, the estate is divided in half.

There are exceptions in which separate or "noncommunity" property is allowed even though one's legal residence may be in a community property state. Here are examples:

- Any assets acquired by either party before marriage. Afterward, the income, profits, and improvements relating to such property may be considered community property.
- Gifts or inheritance, even during the marriage.

- Earnings of a wife while she is separated from her husband (in some states only).
- Compensation received by an injured partner.

People residing in community property states should be aware of three things:

1. *The importance of accurate records,* especially of property acquired in a noncommunity property state. Recognizing that there may be confusion as to who owns what, these states have statutes that, in effect, say that when there's doubt as to ownership, the property must be considered jointly owned.

2. *Many community property states are retirement areas to which older people move.* Frequently, these retirees have accumulated most of their wealth in noncommunity, common-law states. Generally, such assets do not become joint property at change of residence, but this is not always true.

   In California, for instance, the law states that unless certain legal precautions are taken, a surviving spouse may claim the absolute right to inherit half of the decedent's estate. This holds regardless of whether such assets were acquired in a noncommunity property state and even though the decedent may have planned (but not in writing) to leave them to someone else.

3. *The community property state provisions may apply even if the parties later move to a noncommunity property state or foreign country.*

Advice: If you are going to move to or from a community property state, see a lawyer immediately to be sure that your estate plan fulfills your objectives under the law of your new home.

3. Subject to Beneficiary Designation. The transfer at death takes place according to a "beneficiary designation." It is automatic and does not depend on a will or probate.

With life insurance, for example, the owner of the policy names one or more persons or organizations to receive the proceeds at the owner's death. When the policyholder dies, the insurance company makes the payment directly to the beneficiary or beneficiaries as stated in the policy's beneficiary provisions.

This procedure is also followed with the proceeds of most pension and profit-sharing plans. If the employee dies before retirement, the benefits are paid as designated by the individual employee.

Note that unless specifically made payable to the estate, such properties do *not* pass through the deceased's estate and are not subject to the terms of a will or, when there is no will, to the requirements of state laws.

4. Held in Trust. This type of ownership is discussed in detail later, but broadly speaking, a trust is a written agreement that puts property under the direction of a trustee. At some future time, often beyond the life of the person establishing the trust, the agreement is terminated and the property involved distributed to the designated beneficiary or beneficiaries.

Holding property in trust is a means of ownership, similar to the ownership of an insurance policy in that the property is ultimately distributed to beneficiaries designated by the one establishing the trust and is not usually subject to the terms of that person's will or the probate process. Many trusts involve tax savings.

ACQUISITION OF PROPERTY

Property is acquired in different ways:

- With savings, by purchase alone, or in partnership with others.
- With profits on investments.
- On credit such as a mortgage.
- Through gifts and/or inheritances.

As you'll learn in the chapters ahead, there are many ways to plan your estate to make the disposition of property easier and less expensive, and the property itself less heavily taxed.

Remember

1. Ownership means *possession* and *control of enjoyment.*
2. Property is either *real* or *personal.*
3. Personal property is either *tangible* or *intangible.*
4. Property may be owned alone (sole name) or with others.
5. Shared ownership means: tenancy in common, joint tenancy

(with right of survivorship), tenancy by the entireties, partnership, community property.

6. Insurance and retirement rights are often subject to beneficiary designation.

7. Property held in trust passes according to a written trust document.

8. Property passes at the death of the owner in accordance with a will, probate laws, right of survivorship, beneficiary designation, or the terms of a trust—it all depends on how it is held.

2

Your will

How often the question is asked: "Why do I need an attorney to help me write a will? I know what I want." The answer is simple: You do not need an attorney to help you write your will. You can do it yourself. But people who do can create serious problems causing their heirs financial loss.

There's the story about the man who wrote his own will and merely said, "I leave everything to Mom." What could be clearer? It seemed, however, he had had the habit during his lifetime of referring to his wife as "Mom," and to complicate matters, he was survived by his wife and his mother.

There is a toast each year at the British Bar Convention. It is to the person who prepares his own will. So often litigation results from homemade wills, and litigation, of course, is what lawyers thrive on.

A VALID WILL

A will has to comply with the laws of the state within which the person making the will resides at the time it is signed. The laws of the various states are not uniform. But as a general principle, it can be said that in most states a will is valid if it is signed by one of legal age before two witnesses of legal age and if at the time it is so signed the person making the will declares in the presence of the witnesses that the instrument is his last will and testament and he wants them to act as witnesses to his will. He then signs the will and the witnesses then sign, all in the presence of each other. Normally, only the original of the will is signed, for the reason that if it is revoked or changed in the future, there is only one original instrument to look for.

9

Most states have laws that provide that a will validly entered into by a person in another state will be recognized in the state within which the person making the will dies even if that state's law of execution is different.

A properly drawn will should dispose of everything. A person's assets change during his lifetime. It is very unusual for a person to die with exactly the same assets he owned at the time he made his will. It generally is not good technique to designate specific assets to specific beneficiaries. For instance, if you want to give a son stock in XYZ corporation worth $5,000, it would be better to give him a specific amount of $5,000. You may not own any shares of XYZ corporation when you die.

There are exceptions to the rule. For instance, you have a business. This item might be mentioned specifically.

All properly prepared wills have what is called a residuary clause. A residuary clause is one that, after you have designated certain specific items or amounts to go to certain persons, states: "I give and devise all of the rest, residue, and remainder of my estate of whatever kind and whatsoever nature to my ———." Or the residuary clause might read: "I give and devise all of the rest, residue, and remainder of my estate 10% thereof to my son, John, if he survives me and if he does not survive me then to his children who do survive me by right of representation; 10% thereof to my daughter, Mary," etc.

There are, of course, many, many different ways of writing wills. A well-drafted will provides for all contingencies, particularly the contingency of what is to happen in the event that the person you want to have some portion of your estate does not survive you. Sometimes a special survival provision is in the will to the effect that in order for a person to take under your will, he or she must survive you by a certain period of time—e.g., thirty days.

There oftentimes is what is called the simultaneous death clause, a clause that provides for what is to happen if you and your spouse die under such circumstances that it is not possible to determine which of you died first—for instance, if you were both killed in an airplane accident. The clause would provide a presumption that one survived the other—and the decision as to which is presumed to survive probably would be based on tax considerations.

An important part of a will is the tax clause—the clause that provides for payment of the death taxes, if any. Of major concern in many cases is the structuring of language in the tax clause of a will to make sure the assets are left in such a way as to minimize federal estate taxes and state inheritance or estate taxes.

One of the most important parts of a will is that which nominates the person or organization that is to act as your personal representative (in some states referred to as the executor). Your personal representative can be anyone of legal age or it can be a professional such as a bank or trust company authorized by law to act as such (see Chapter 9).

In many instances, a will is the most important document a person ever signs. No thinking person would want to take a chance on such an important document being defective, with the possible result that the persons you intended to receive your wealth do not get it.

WHO SHOULD BE WITNESSES TO A WILL?

If you have been asked to be a witness to someone's will, chances are you are not a beneficiary in the will. Though many states have now changed their laws so that a witness to a will can also be a beneficiary in the will, there are still many state laws that specifically provide that a witness to a will either takes nothing under the will or that the share of the witness is limited to the amount the witness would have received if the person died without a will—and often this is nothing.

Even in states that allow witnesses to take under the will, it is better procedure to have persons witness the will that are not in any way beneficiaries under the will. Generally, the lawyer who prepares a will acts as one of the witnesses. In most states the witnesses have to be of legal age—age eighteen in some states, age twenty-one in others.

It is a good idea for the witnesses to the will to be younger than the person signing the will. The obvious reason for this is that in case of disputes after the death of the one signing the will, it is most helpful if the person who witnessed the will is alive and able to testify as to what went on at the time the will was signed.

WHAT MAKES A WILL INVALID?

A will that is not signed and properly witnessed is invalid. Assuming the will has been properly signed and witnessed and disposes of all assets, it still may be invalidated, at least in part, if:

1. It violates certain statutory rights of the maker's heirs at law. For instance, in most states, a surviving spouse—unless during the lifetime of the person whose will is being challenged that spouse properly waived his or her statutory rights—will be entitled to certain sums out of the estate of the deceased spouse, generally from one third to one half of the estate.

2. It can be established that the will was procured by fraud or the decedent was subject to undue influence—fraud and undue influence are very closely related in will contest litigation.

3. It can be established that the decedent was not competent at the time the will was signed. Competency to make a valid last will and testament is generally not the same competency as is required in signing, for instance, a complicated contract. In most states, all that really is necessary to determine that the person signing the will was competent is to establish that that person knew the objects of his or her bounty, had a general idea of the extent of his or her wealth, and at the time the instrument was signed intended that the persons designated in the instrument be the ones to receive his or her wealth.

BUT IT'S NOT FAIR

How often we hear omitted heirs say that the will was not fair. Fairness hasn't a thing to do with it. If the person signing the will was of sound and disposing mind at the time he or she signed the will, was not under any undue influence, if no statutory rights were violated and the will was validly signed and witnessed, then that will will be honored by the court, even though the judge might totally agree with an omitted heir that the will was not fair.

Sometimes persons who take care of and have genuine regard for a particular person are not adequately provided for in that person's will. Relief can be achieved by making a claim in the estate of the deceased person for services rendered, but oftentimes those claims are difficult to prove and if proved, the amount received does not adequately compensate the omitted person for all of his or her efforts.

Persons of wealth have been known to lead others on with such statements as: "Don't worry; you will be taken care of in my will." But then, when that person dies, the promise has not been fulfilled in the will. Perhaps the promise was false. Perhaps late in life something happened whereby the person was offended, often inadvertently or mistakenly, and the will was changed to cut out a beneficiary. In most states, even if the decedent was mistaken about a situation that caused him or her to change the will and eliminate a particular beneficiary, the courts still will honor the document and that beneficiary will take only what the will provides, if anything.

HOW DO I CHANGE MY WILL?

One can change a will as many times as one wants. It is only the will that is in effect at the time of death that controls. If the change is a short one, it can be accomplished by what is called a codicil. The word "codicil" really means "amendment."

But remember, the codicil has to be signed with the same formality as a will. Under no circumstances should a valid will, after it has been properly signed and witnessed, be scratched out, modified, or in any other way changed, because to do so will perhaps invalidate the whole instrument or, as a bare minimum, result in confusions that may require court interpretations or maybe even litigation.

STATUTORY RIGHTS—PREMARITAL AGREEMENTS

As stated above, most surviving spouses have certain statutory rights in the decedent's estate unless during the decedent's lifetime the surviving spouse waived his or her rights.

How can these rights be waived? Often they are waived by what is called an "antenuptial" or "premarital" agreement. For instance, it is not uncommon for parties to a second marriage, particularly when both have families from prior marriages, to enter into a premarital agreement whereby, in consideration of the pending marriage, each waives statutory rights in the property of the other, to the end that if either dies, property can be left to whomever he or she chooses without any requirement to comply with statutory provisions for a surviving spouse.

Antenuptial agreements sometimes are valid only if they are entered into prior to marriage. Generally, the parties to the antenuptial agreement have to make a full disclosure to each other of the extent of their assets. Also, it is best if the parties to the agreement are represented by different lawyers.

Antenuptial agreements are awkward. They are entered into at a time when love is in the air and the parties to the contract are often planning their marriage. Affirming trust in each other, they state that all they want from each other is love and not property.

It is not uncommon, even though an antenuptial agreement has been entered into, to also have a waiver of statutory rights signed at the same time wills are prepared for the newlyweds. It is sort of "frosting on the cake." It really is not necessary that consents to new wills be signed.

After marriage, if the parties have failed to sign a premarital agreement, it still is possible in certain states for them to enter into a valid antenuptial agreement; but after the marriage, there is obviously not the same incentive for the spouse with few assets to sign away any of his or her rights to the more substantial assets of the other spouse.

In some states, antenuptial agreements can also provide for waiver of alimony, support, and property settlement if the marriage does not work out and ends in divorce. In fact, such agreements are sometimes used in sophisticated "live-in lover" situations.

HANDWRITTEN WILLS

There are states where a person can write out and sign, without any witnesses, a valid will if he does it all in his own handwriting. Not too many states still recognize such so-called holographic wills, however.

Perhaps the most famous situation of this kind is the Howard Hughes situation. At last count, there were over thirty alleged holographic wills by Howard Hughes! So far, none of them have been determined to be valid.

The authors are totally opposed to holographic wills. For instance, a person is in the hospital, upset because none of his relatives are visiting him, and decides to leave everything to his nurse, who is taking such good care of him. The patient writes out a will accordingly and forgets about it. Five years later he dies, and the writing turns up, leaving everything to the nurse. Not fair, perhaps, but it would control if the state the person lived in honored holographic wills.

A will is a very serious document and in the judgment of the authors it should be signed before witnesses with certain formalities accomplished at the time of signing.

Understand that a will can be handwritten as well as typewritten.

A holographic will is one that is totally handwritten and signed by the person making the will without witnesses. A handwritten will signed before two witnesses who also signed the document, all in the presence of each other, is just as good as a typewritten instrument properly signed and witnessed.

There are other examples of famous handwritten wills besides the Howard Hughes fiasco. There is the story about the farmer whose tractor tipped over on him; knowing he was going to die, he managed to scratch out on the fender of the tractor that he left everything to his wife. That was accomplished in a state that allowed holographic wills and the fender of the tractor was then duly admitted to probate.

Or take the actual incident of the person who, choking on his food in a restaurant, had the presence to scratch his will on a napkin before the required witnesses, and then he died. The napkin was duly admitted to probate as a valid last will and testament of the person who choked to death.

DOES A WILL AVOID PROBATE?

For some reason, many people think that a valid will eliminates probate. It does not. A valid will does assure that the designated persons will receive the estate. Most important, it designates who is to handle the decedent's affairs. (See Chapter 3: "What is probate?")

IF I HAVE EVERYTHING IN JOINT TENANCY, WHY DO I NEED A WILL?

You never know who is going to survive. If you have everything in joint tenancy with your spouse and your spouse dies a few minutes before you, then it is all yours and you should have a will to designate what is to happen in that event. See Chapter 4: "The Truth About Joint Tenancy."

WHERE SHOULD I KEEP MY WILL?

The answer to this is: a safe place. We usually recommend that it *not* be put in a safe-deposit box, because it is possible that after death, under the laws of your state your safe-deposit box may be sealed until the local officials can inventory its contents to make sure that all the assets of the deceased person are reported for death-tax purposes. It is aggravating to survivors to have to go through this routine—most people look on it as an intrusion by government. For this reason, we usually recommend that a copy of the will be placed in a safe-deposit box but that the original be kept some other place—for instance, at your lawyer's office, in a safe place at home, or with the professional organization nominated as personal representative. If the instrument is lost or destroyed by fire, your lawyer can always use his copy to "prove up a lost or destroyed will."

3

What is probate?

The word *"probate"* strikes fear in the hearts of those who hear it, yet few people understand the term. Writers have become rich trying to tell people how to avoid it, and property owners go to great lengths to stay away from it. All too often, attempts to avoid probate have resulted in the wrong people receiving property and the right ones having to pay heavy and unnecessary estate and inheritance taxes.

Probate is not a monster created by unscrupulous lawyers and fostered by corrupt judges. It has a great deal of validity and, perhaps for that reason, has lasted for centuries.

The term *probate* is generally used to signify an important part of a court system that exists in the fifty states and in all countries of the free world. It refers to the process that governs the administration and distribution of property belonging to persons who have died. It also means the enforcement of the terms of a person's last will or ensuring adherence to laws concerning the distribution of property for a person who has died without a will.

To the layman, probate may appear to be a slow, cumbersome, and expensive process. For that reason, some people argue that it should be updated and simplified. We agree wholeheartedly. In fact, probate has already been revised in many states. However, no one with any real knowledge of the law governing estates wants the system to be abolished. It works and has proven a powerful legal safeguard for millions of people.

Probate property is real estate, securities, jewelry, automobiles, art, coins, and other assets held in the name of an individual *alone.* There is no predetermination by trust, joint tenancy, or beneficiary as to how the property will pass at death.

17

After demise, the distribution of the property is made in accordance with a will if the owner dies with a valid last testament. When there is no acceptable will, the estate passes by what is known as "intestate" law, under which the pattern of distribution is dictated by statute.

With or without a will, every estate held by a person in his own name must go through probate. What this means is that *everybody has a will whether or not he knows it.* If you are not prudent enough to prepare a last testament, the state provides a ready-made will under intestate law.

If you want your property to go to a specific individual, you should have a valid will (one properly drawn and accepted by the court). If you do not leave such a document, the court must act according to the law, which may require that your property be distributed in a manner entirely different from what you desire. The probate court, in effect, is a referee in the allocation of your estate, either in accordance with your will if you leave one or in accordance with state law if you die without a valid will. If you die without a will or your will is proved invalid and no relatives can be located, your property escheats to the state.

DEATH WITHOUT A WILL

Among Americans who die each year, more than 70 percent leave no will. Wives and single people are especially remiss in this area. Unfortunately, not leaving a will can have costly consequences.

If you die without a will and heirs survive you, your assets will be distributed by impersonal law under the jurisdiction of a personal representative appointed by the court. He must work within the narrow outlines of statutes designed to provide the greatest good for the greatest number of people. There's little room for sentiment, for following your wishes, or for making allocations according to need.

In most states, if one dies without a will the decedent's spouse will get one third to one half of the decedent's estate and the rest will be split among the children, regardless of their age or circumstances. The same percentage of a man's wealth will go to his seven-year-old son as to his married daughter, or to his affluent son as to his crippled daughter, whom he might have wanted to help to a greater extent.

If you die without a will and no spouse or children or grandchildren survive you, then most state laws will split your property among your parents or the survivor thereof, and if neither survives, then to your brothers and sisters—and if you have no surviving brothers or sisters or nieces and nephews, right on down the line until cousins, second cousins, etc., surface to inherit your wealth.

ROLE OF THE PROBATE COURT

The probate court acts as a referee and decision maker by answering pertinent questions and resolving conflicts of interpretation. In the case of a poorly worded will, the question might be: "What did the draftsman mean?" Or the heirs might ask: "Were the terms of the will procured by undue influence?"; "Was the person making the will of sound and disposing mind?"; "Are there indications that the person handling the estate has made a serious mistake or is guilty of embezzlement?"; "Who makes sure that the estate representative pays the taxes and just debts?"; or "How can a dispute over a debt be resolved?"

Although many probate court functions are more or less routine, there can be occasions when the answers to such questions will be significant to beneficiaries; one example is the decision of the court as to which assets should be sold to make the designated allocations of assets.

TIME AND COST OF PROBATE

The next important and often most alarming questions have to do with how long probate will take and how much it will cost.

Time There are no set answers on time. The length of a probate depends on the nature of the assets, tax problems, and the complexity of the legacies. Probates can take as little as one month if a summary proceeding (a short formal review under the court's jurisdiction) is held, or they can drag out for years if the estate is diverse, tax problems exist, or disputes occur.

Do not be alarmed at the prospect that probate may take as long as three years or more. That length of time is unusual, but it is not necessarily injurious. Often, long periods of probate can be used to secure tax advantages for the beneficiaries. This is because a probate estate is a separate taxpayer. But you should be fully informed by your lawyer as to "why" it is taking so long.

A probate can achieve tax savings in several ways, such as: by delaying distributions to keep income in the estate, which may have a lower income tax rate than the eventual beneficiaries; or by "sprinkling"— a process whereby different sums are paid to different beneficiaries. For example, allocating more income to children, who are subject to a low tax rate, than to a high-tax-bracket adult.

In spite of tax benefits that may be derived, most beneficiaries want to get things over with and push for quick completion of probate. Your attorney will tell you that ending probate promptly is usually best. When probate is protracted, there is always the danger that the Internal Revenue Service will rule that the estate was held open for an unreasonable time and thus may not be eligible for tax savings.

Cost. In the past, the cost of probate was based strictly on the value of the estate. State bar associations often established a schedule of attorney fees expressed as a percentage of estate value: usually from 3 to 4 percent for estates under $500,000, and the dollar fees increasing with the size of the estate but constituting a smaller percentage of total value. Bar Association–mandated fee schedules are no longer used.

There may also be fees due the personal representative, customarily payable according to a preset schedule when it's a financial institution. When the personal representative is a surviving spouse, child, or relative, there's often no fee. If money is paid out, it will be taxable to the recipient as ordinary income at a rate generally higher than that of the estate tax. A professional personal representative, such as a bank or a trust company, will always charge a fee.

The trend in the legal profession has been away from the percentage fee. This is fair to both the lawyer and the client. It isn't necessarily the value of the estate that makes for a more involved probate, although usually there is a definite relationship between size and complexity.

The fees for large estates or those representing extraordinary problems and/or substantial assets in real estate or a business may be negotiated either by the decedent during his or her lifetime or by the decedent's personal representative after death.

Services rendered by the lawyer usually include preparation of estate and income tax returns, processing papers relating to joint tenancy, and other paperwork. Legal fees can be sizable even when everything is in joint tenancy; for example, if the first member of a joint tenancy who dies is the "wrong" one—that is, the person who did not own or contribute to the purchase of jointly owned property—tax disputes may result.

Example: A husband and wife hold in joint tenancy a large parcel of real estate which the husband paid for with an inheritance. If the wife dies first, the husband could have unexpected taxes to pay. He must be able to prove that he alone paid for the real estate. Otherwise, federal and many state authorities will tax the joint tenancy property as though owned by the wife. Contesting such decisions can involve substantial legal expenses.

Sometimes, allowing the property to go through probate can reduce estate and inheritance taxes. Such savings can be accomplished by establishing trusts in a will that become effective after death. This approach can (1) avoid part of the taxes that ordinarily would be due when the beneficiary of a trust dies, and (2) eliminate a second probate at the death of the survivor (see Chapter 6).

As a rule of thumb, the cost of processing nonprobate assets (those not owned in a single name) is about half that of the probate process. Again, this depends on the complexity of the situation.

Some people like the ease of control and simplicity of sole-name ownership even though this can subject all assets to probate. A blanket statement that probate is always to be avoided is simply untrue. The decision to avoid probate should be made only after a careful review of a person's assets and intentions. There are occasions when probate should be avoided and other times when it should be sought. Before taking any action, consult your attorney. And never be fearful of the probate process.

A WILL IS NOT ENOUGH

Making the transition from wife to widow is difficult, but preliminary planning can render the process easier and avoid many future problems. Here are some steps a husband can take to ease the strain of his death:

Keep vital papers in a convenient place. Arrange a handy depository, such as a safe-deposit box, for insurance policies, deeds, securities, contracts, and notes. This will save time and concern in looking for these documents when they are needed.

The original of your will should be filed with your personal representative, if a trust company,* your attorney, or in a safe spot to which there is ready access without legal authorization, such as might be needed with a lock box.

Make certain that adequate liquid assets are available. There should be ready cash and easily converted assets for payments of debts, taxes, and living expenses of the survivors. These can be in the form of life insurance, negotiable securities, or cash in a separate bank or savings account. If there are not sufficient liquid assets, it will be necessary to sell some property, probably at an unfavorable price and possibly incurring additional taxes.

Have an attorney who is familiar with your estate, your will, and your family needs. It's also a good idea to make informal arrangements about the anticipated legal fees.

Write general instructions, describing how you would like personal effects, such as clothes, jewelry, and mementos, disposed of. Do not clutter your will with such specifics. Then attach this informal note to your will. Some states have laws that give legal significance to such instructions, and even in states that don't usually your wishes will be respected by your personal representative.

Treat your spouse as a partner in family financial affairs. Keep your spouse informed about investments, company benefit plans, pension programs, insurance, and other estate plans.

Review your will periodically. A will should be checked periodically to make sure that the provisions conform with changing federal and state laws and your own resources and wishes. Since he will be familiar with your needs, try to schedule this review with the same lawyer who drew your will if you are satisfied with his ability as an estate planner.

---

*If a bank or trust company is named in the will as Personal Representative, i.e., Executor it will provide storage for the original free of charge.

GUARDIANSHIP/CONSERVATORSHIP

In addition to supervising the administration of decedents' estates, probate courts supervise the administration of the estates of minors and persons who lack the capacity to handle their own affairs. This category of responsibilities is known as guardianship or conservatorship. It is a fact that as people grow older, their ability to administer business affairs and investments diminishes. In some cases, the decrease is so severe that the individual is unable to handle routine matters, such as banking and record-keeping. In many of these cases, it is necessary to request the court to appoint a suitable guardian or conservator to assist the incapacitated individual. The guardian or conservator must prepare an inventory and file it with the court. Often, a bond is also required to assure the guardian's performance. Periodically, usually annually, he must show all receipts and disbursements for that period. At the death of the incapacitated person, a final account is prepared and submitted to the court. Upon the court's approval, the guardian or conservator is discharged and the assets turned over to the personal representative of the decedent.

The difference between a guardianship and a conservatorship is that in a conservatorship there is no determination of incompetency. We all know of people who are not incompetent but who still need help in handling their affairs—protection from artful and deceitful persons who might take advantage of their lack of ability to handle their own affairs. In both guardianship and conservatorship, there is total involvement by the probate court in the administration of the subject's affairs.

The law of guardianship must contemplate a wide range of skills and quality of judgment among those appointed guardian. Hence, these laws are necessarily restrictive, requiring court approval before investments can be made, for example. Also, the ward's business affairs are exposed to public scrutiny, since all matters related to the guardianship must be filed with the court.

Families who find themselves in these circumstances sometimes try to avoid guardianship through means which often are not effective or satisfactory. For example, occasionally an elderly person will grant a power of attorney to a spouse, child, or friend. Although some states have passed laws allowing these powers to remain in force after the person granting them has become mentally incompetent (durable powers of attorney), the basic rule is that such powers terminate upon the death or incapacity of the person giving them. In any event, most banks and others in the financial community are reluctant to conduct substantial transactions on the basis of powers of attorney. Durable powers of attorney should be granted only to a person who is most trusted.

Sometimes a person will add a trusted party, such as a child or a friend, as a cosigner or joint tenant on bank accounts. The purpose is to allow the cosigner to make withdrawals and expenditures for the benefit of the owner of the account. Unfortunately, at the death of the owner, the cosigner receives the balance of the account by operation of law, which may not have been the intention of the owner and, in fact, may conflict with his general estate plan.

In some circumstances, usually involving modest estates, guardianship or conservatorship may be the only solution. But in cases where estates are more substantial, the creation of an inter vivos trust is much better if competency is not a problem. Here the transition of administration from owner to trustee can be smooth, private, and without the expenses of a bond and the restrictions of guardianship law.

4

The truth about joint tenancy

Many people believe that the use of joint tenancy is always the wisest course. They like dual ownership because it allows them to manage their assets and because of the relative ease with which property can be transferred at death. Joint tenancy can accomplish a lot of good, but it's like a doctor's prescription: It should be taken in the proper dosage.

After years of experience in estate planning and settlement, we believe that there is no pat formula that can be applied to all situations. Joint ownership can be useful, but it can also cause difficulties. Questions can arise regarding control of assets during life and taxes after death. Often, the problems do not occur until many years after the original registration, usually when one of the joint tenants has died.

Always consult a lawyer before you decide on joint ownership of anything, be it a home, a condominium, commercial real estate, securities, savings, or even a checking account.

In estate planning, most husbands and wives have similar goals. They want to be sure that in case of death, the survivor will be well provided for, and that when the survivor dies, what is left will go, quickly and easily, to the children.

Joint tenancy may be the wise course in specific situations, but each decision regarding ownership should be made on the basis of a review of the total picture: all your assets, your family circumstances, your overall estate plan, and tax considerations.

If you asked a bank or a savings and loan association how best to set up a $10,000 inheritance, chances are that you would be advised to establish the account in joint tenancy between you and your spouse. It would probably be explained to you that if you died, your spouse would get the money automatically, without the necessity of probate.

This could be wise counsel; it would depend on the nature and extent of your other assets and on your estate planning intentions.

One thing is sure: If the advice is good advice, it was by accident. The officer in charge of savings accounts would never be so presumptuous as to inquire into your other assets, your family's financial background and needs, or your own plan for your estate after death—all the data necessary for sound advice. His responsibility is limited to advising you on the various plans offered by his institution.

In our experience, joint tenancy is suitable for the household checking account, small savings accounts, and title to your home. It provides:

A sense of family security. It's a partnership that gives a feeling of greater group security, unity, and harmony than it is possible to get with individual ownership.

Convenience. Bank accounts in joint tenancy can be easily liquidated or drawn upon, by either co-owner, for emergency needs.

Protection of property from claims after death. In many states, certain jointly owned property is not subject to claims made by creditors of the deceased co-owner.

This exemption can also apply to damage/injury claims. If one joint tenant dies as the result of an automobile accident in which he was at fault, and the insurance coverage was inadequate, a judgment exceeding the insurance policy limit could not be collected against assets held in joint tenancy.

Avoidance of publicity. Prompt transfer of ownership can be completed without the publicity that may accompany the probate of a will.

Reduction of estate administration costs. Since ownership of joint tenancy property passes automatically to the co-owner at the death of the other partner, administration expenses are not applicable to that part of the estate when probated under a will. This eliminates a lot of legal hocus-pocus and can mean lower settlement bills.

DISADVANTAGES OF JOINT TENANCY

Some of the negative aspects of joint tenancy include:

Loss of control. In most cases, joint tenancy reduces a person's legal control over property. If you have a joint bank account and become ill, the other joint tenant can withdraw sums of money against that account without your knowledge or consent. You may wake up one morning to find that your spouse has withdrawn all of your money and left town—and there's nothing you can do about it!

Need for complete agreement. Decisions on how jointly held property is to be used, managed, and invested must be made harmoniously. Such unanimity can be difficult to achieve if there's a divorce, separation, or intrafamily dispute. For example:

- At the time of property settlement discussions in the event of the divorce, your spouse may demand your share of the joint tenancy on the grounds that the other half is hers already and so should not be involved in the negotiations.
- You and your son own your home together. You both agree to sell, but your son's wife says no. Under some circumstances, she may be able to stop the transaction because of her interest in her husband's real estate.
- You and your daughter jointly own stock. You want to sell, but she refuses to sign the certificates. There's no way to complete the sale without resorting to legal action.

Loss of right to dispose of property at death. A person who places property in joint ownership usually gives up the right to dispose of it in his will. This is so even though you state in your last testament that all your property is to go to someone other than the co-owner. You may have set up the joint tenancy as a matter of convenience while you were incapacitated, but with no intention that the surviving joint tenant should receive all your property at your death. However, if you die while in the hospital, the other owner may very well get every dime in that joint account, and a legal fight is almost sure to follow.

What it comes down to is that you can have the fanciest will in town, but if everything you own is set up in joint tenancy, in all probability the will isn't worth the paper it's written on, since joint tenancy usually takes precedence. As already pointed out, if you leave your assets in joint ownership and simultaneously dispose of them in some other way in your will, there may be a court battle.

There are exceptions, but as a rule, joint tenancy property is presumed to have been owned *entirely* by the first joint tenant who dies: not half, but *all*. This presumption can be overcome only by proof that the property or some portion of it was paid for by the survivor from his own money and that it was placed in joint tenancy solely for convenience. Each share should be clearly identified if both individuals contributed to the purchase.

The fact that property is in joint tenancy does not mean that legal procedures can be completely avoided when one of the joint tenants dies. The title to the property will have to be cleared. The name of the person who has died must be removed from the title. This often requires the filing of affidavits and death certificates, and sometimes obtaining tax clearance.

The question of ownership becomes especially important when the joint tenant who did not contribute to the purchase of the property dies first and taxing authorities propose to tax the full value of all such property in his or her estate. This can become very complex.

Example: Mr. and Mrs. Doremus were both employed. Mr. Doremus bought stocks with his own money and put the shares in joint ownership with his wife. When the price of the stocks advanced, he sold at a profit and deposited the proceeds in a joint checking account. Later, he used this money to buy another stock, which he listed in both names.

When Mrs. Doremus died, there was a question as to how much of the jointly owned securities were part of her taxable estate. The tax authorities said all of it was "because the husband was unable to prove it was his money that was used in the purchase of the stocks."

This question of contribution becomes very important when joint ownership continues over a long period of time.

Example: At age twenty-seven, when he had more hopes than assets, Dr. Smith drew a will that left everything to his wife. Twenty years later, he has a $150,000 home and securities worth $350,000: a total of $500,000, all in joint tenancy with his spouse.

The good doctor believes that since his wife owns half of the assets, the $250,000 marital deduction, applicable to the estate of the first partner to die, would reduce his taxable estate to zero (see Chapter 7). *He's wrong, because his wife contributed virtually nothing. (Note:* Dr. Smith would probably be right if he lived in a community property state.)

If he should die after 1980 (when the federal estate tax credit reaches a maximum under the 1976 Tax Reform Act), his estate would be taxable by the federal government and the tax would be $21,400, or 4.3 percent of his estate. On the subsequent death of his wife, assuming she has kept the value of what she received from her husband, the entire estate would be taxed again, at a higher rate, because there would be no marital deduction. This time the federal tax bite would be about $92,000, or 18.4 percent of her estate.

Without joint tenancy, Dr. Smith could leave his widow half of his wealth and put the balance in a trust that would not become part of her taxable estate. He could save about $71,000 in federal taxes alone!

The above example only discusses the federal estate tax. State inheritance and estate taxes would be additional. The Smiths have substantial potential death taxes that they should seek to avoid.

Possible gift taxes. Establishing joint tenancy can also subject the transaction to gift taxes. If you purchase securities or real estate and then place title in joint ownership with someone else, you may have to pay a gift tax on one half of the value of the property. Under IRS interpretation, the gift tax takes effect when one person becomes entitled to more than he put in.

There can also be trouble in the future if you decide to sever the joint ownership. You may then get hit with another gift tax, this time on the half of the property you previously gave away. It all depends.

There is one important exception to jointly held property subject to gift taxes: stocks in street-name brokerage accounts (held by the broker). If either joint owner can deal with the account alone and make withdrawals without the consent of the other, no gift tax is imposed until the noncontributor withdraws completely. Another exception pertains to real estate placed in joint tenancy between married persons. No gift results unless the married couple makes an election to have the transaction considered a gift.

Under all circumstances, when you are considering entering into or

*withdrawing from joint tenancy, consult a lawyer to make sure you
do not run afoul of tax laws.*

LIMITED JOINT TENANCY When the total value of property is modest (say a $10,000 bank account or a $50,000 home) there is probably
no reason why both should not be held in joint tenancy. If anything
happens to either spouse, the survivor will need the money and the
house.

With substantial estates—say, a net worth, including life insurance
death proceeds, of over $300,000—joint tenancy with a spouse gener-
ally should be limited to the homestead and household checking accounts. One reason for this suggestion is the problem of management.

This kind of estate involves a sizable sum. In most cases, a homemaker has done a good job handling income, but she has not had much
experience with principal. Now, all of a sudden, when circumstances
and grief may cloud her ability to reason clearly, she must manage a
lot of money. She has almost complete freedom to do with it whatever
she wishes.

In many cases she may be inexperienced, and usually she will be
under pressure from relatives anxious to share her grief (and the
assets). They think they want to protect the assets from unscrupulous
promoters, and from well-meaning but often impractical friends. Her
brother may urge her to buy shares in a South American get-rich-
quick scheme or, with a little encouragement from her neighbors, she
may decide to fulfill her dreams and splurge with a remodeled
kitchen, a new vacation home, or an around-the-world trip.

There's nothing wrong with a widow using some of her assets for any
legitimate expenditure, as long as she realizes her financial limitations
and fulfills her responsibilities to the children. Many women do a
better job of managing money than their husbands did. But almost
everyone can benefit from the counsel and cautionary advice of a
competent lawyer or a professional trustee named in a will or provided through an agreement entered into during the husband's lifetime.

Joint tenancy and estate tax savings. The time to avoid estate taxes
is *before* death. Too many people delay, or refuse to take, protective
steps such as providing a trust either during their lifetime or to become effective at death. Once a person has received property out-

right, as a surviving joint tenant, the only way by which estate taxes can then be reduced is by making gifts, which, in turn, may now be subject to costly taxes.

If a man has a $350,000 estate, he could establish trusts that would make certain that his widow, while she lives, would have the economic benefit from his property, and, at her death, she would be able to pass the principal on to her children without any federal estate tax being imposed at either the husband's death or the subsequent demise of the wife.

By employing refinements of this trust technique, the Rockefellers, Kennedys, and other wealthy families have been successful in avoiding debilitating taxes for generations. However, the 1976 Tax Reform Act now taxes "generation-skipping" trusts.

You may say, "Yes, that's O.K. for the very rich, but I'm not in that league." In many cases, this is not true: You may be in that league and not know it! The 1976 tax law raised the figure for minimum taxable estate, but, as we'll outline later, even modest estates can be subject to unnecessary taxes unless the assets are protected by a trust.

Wealthy people may be able to save more dollars on taxes than you can, but they are also in a better position to pay them. People with modest estates who save a few thousand tax dollars benefit far more percentagewise than do their rich counterparts. Sit down with your lawyer or tax adviser and see for yourself. For tax reasons alone, look hard at joint tenancy and make certain that the savings in probate expenses are not outweighed by unnecessary taxes.

No substitute for a will. Many people think that one of the big advantages of joint ownership is that it eliminates the bother and expense of making a will. This is partially true at times, but more often, it can be faulty—and costly—reasoning.

ARE THERE ANY ALTERNATIVES?

Durable power of attorney. Your mother is getting on in years. Your father died some years ago. Mom has about $100,000 in savings accounts and certificates of deposit, primarily from the sale of the homestead. It was getting to be too much for her. She now lives in an apartment, but because of the infirmities of advancing years, she is fearful of having to go into a medical care facility and if something like that does happen to her, she wants to make sure her funds are properly handled. She has three children and she wants her estate to go to them equally. A good friend of hers has just given her some advice. The friend said that she should put all her assets into joint tenancy with her daughter, the one who lives the closest to her and is the most attentive to her, so that the daughter can handle her affairs and spend the money for her during her lifetime. Your mother just received some bad advice—well-meaning but, all the same, bad advice.

What should she do? She should keep her assets in her own name, have a will prepared for her that leaves her estate equally to her three children, and give the attentive daughter a durable power of attorney.

All states have laws that in effect provide that one person may give another person a power of attorney to act in his place. All that is necessary is that the person be competent at the time he or she is giving the power of attorney. Until recently, many states had laws that provided that when a person became incompetent, the power of attorney previously granted was no longer valid.

A number of states have adopted what is called a durable power of attorney. The word "durable" means that all that is necessary is that the person granting the power be competent at the time of the grant, and should the person later on become incompetent, the power of attorney continues in existence.

It can be seen that a durable power of attorney is exactly "what the doctor ordered" for older persons. It can serve as a guardianship or conservatorship substitute as well as a good alternative to joint tenancy.

Powers of attorney can be very restrictive or very broad. Usually, when a durable power of attorney is granted it is a broad power of attorney. This means that the person acting under the power of attorney will have the broadest authority to handle the affairs of the person making the grant.

One word of caution. Because most durable powers of attorney are broad, they should only be granted to someone you thoroughly trust.

Totten trust. Assume a husband and wife who have both worked have accumulated savings of $200,000. Rather than put their savings in joint tenancy, it might be prudent for them to take the savings that they feel are attributable to their earnings and each set them up for the other in a Totten trust.

A Totten trust is nothing more than a "payable on death" bank account. The bank account will usually read "John Doe in trust for Mary Doe." It means that if John Doe dies, the bank account belongs to Mary Doe. Mary Doe would take her separate funds and set them up as "Mary Doe in trust for John Doe," and then if Mary Doe dies, they will pass to John Doe. Everything is kept separate. The beneficiary has no right to the funds in the account of the other until the death of the person who established it. Savings accounts, saving certificates, and most mutual funds can be registered in this manner.

We repeat: Before you consider joint tenancy for any property, consult a lawyer and make your decision on the basis of your total present and projected assets, your family circumstances and needs, and your overall estate planning. And do it *now.*

5

Trusts

A	Manage property for you and your family
TRUST	**Extend beyond your lifetime**
CAN	**Keep your financial affairs private**
	Save taxes

In the legal agreement known as a trust, assets are turned over to someone else to hold and manage for the benefit of yourself or a third party. Trusts, in varying forms, can be used to avoid or postpone taxes, to preserve the privacy of an individual's estate, and to provide a means of controlling or administering property.

The first trusts were created centuries ago in England to disguise the actual ownership of property in order to circumvent feudal obligations and laws. A man would convey real estate to another person under a private arrangement which provided that the benefits from the property would flow to the creator of the trust while the legal ownership was held by the trustee.

The trust agreement is a written document that details the manner in which the trustee is to hold the property, the purpose for which its income and principal are to be used, and the duration of the arrangement. In a sense, the trustee is a kind of manager responsible for the care and maintenance of the property, collection of income, and conduct of all business associated with the property; finally, and most importantly, the trustee must account for the administration of the trust to the trustor and/or beneficiaries. The trustee is a fiduciary. The trustee owes a high degree of responsibility to the one creating the trust and to the beneficiaries of the trust.

Some trusts can be established by filling out a printed form, but it is always best to have the agreement prepared by a lawyer experienced in estate planning and probate. There are technical details relating to ownership, taxes, and control of the property that an attorney will be better equipped to deal with than a layman. Some states

34

have laws that limit the trustee's powers and rights and set ranges for fees.

The trustee is paid from the income or assets of the trust, but if he so desires, he can waive compensation. To be safe, have your attorney spell out exactly what the trustee can and cannot do. And to be doubly safe, designate a successor trustee who would be able to take over in case of the first trustee's resignation, death, or disability.

There are no rules limiting the size of a trust. A trust can be for a sum as small as $10,000 or as large as $100 million. Because of the expense of preparation and maintenance, there are, of course, practical minimums. A simple trust can be set up in a short time for a modest fee. More complicated agreements, involving huge sums or special conditions, can require weeks of work and thus be expensive in dollars. But usually these costs will not be significant in relation to the assets in the trust.

State laws vary in detail, but the same broad principles apply. *The measure of a worthwhile trust is its purpose, not the cost of drawing it or the assets involved.*

ADVANTAGES OF A TRUST

It delays and controls distribution of property after death. The trust affords a means of avoiding the problems that arise when beneficiaries are not in a position to handle their inheritance at the time of the donor's demise. The management of property requires judgments regarding investments, expenditures of income and principal, tax planning, accounting, and safekeeping. Not all beneficiaries are able to perform these functions. The trust can provide as little or as much as the creator of the trust thinks wise.

If a man has a will drawn to provide for outright distribution to his heirs, his estate will be allocated according to its terms. The distribution is made after all claims, taxes, and other expenses have been paid. Whether this takes place in a few months or several years depends on the complexity of the estate and the tax problems if any. The age of the heirs is always a significant factor.

Example: Mr. Baxter's beneficiaries are his seventy-five-year-old mother, who is in poor health, his sixteen-year-old son, still unable to handle money well, and his eight-year-old daughter.

A simple will might provide that each of the beneficiaries receive an outright inheritance upon completion of the probate process. But then the problems begin.

The elderly woman may not be able to care for herself, much less her share of the estate, possibly resulting in the worsening of her health and adversely affecting the value of the inheritance. If she is judged legally incompetent, the court will have to appoint a guardian before that share of the property can be sold or mortgaged or its income reinvested.

The inheritance of the son will usually be held in guardianship until he comes of legal age. In many states, majority is now attained at age eighteen, ready or not!

The young daughter will have to have a guardian named to care for her and her property. And even if she is unable to manage her assets when she is legally an adult, the guardianship will probably terminate.

Guardianships rarely last beyond minority, except when an individual is mentally incompetent or completely dependent.

Trusts can solve all these problems. They can provide for responsible administration and management until the death of the grandmother and until the children are able to take control. Under the trust agreement, each beneficiary would receive all the funds available for support and/or education.

A trust is valuable when it comes to children because it assures that they will receive the benefits of the estate without giving them control. If you have qualms about a youngster's management ability, you can arrange for the trustee to be responsible until the child reaches whatever age you set.

This raises a perplexing question: What is the proper age for children to receive an inheritance? The answer to that question will depend on the individuals involved, but here are some guidelines:

Legally, the child becomes an adult at eighteen, nineteen, or twenty-one, according to the law of the state of residence. If the trust entails large sums, it may be that the young person may be forced to accept more responsibility than he or she can handle. For example, your son may have done a good job handling small sums but have no experience in investment or money management. Furthermore, he may be at an age when personal pressures weigh him down. Perhaps he is completing his college education and making a career choice, or planning marriage or postgraduate training. His decision may mean geographic relocation to an area where he will not be able to consult relatives or family friends.

One solution that can be good for almost everyone is to arrange for an installment distribution of the trust: perhaps 10 percent now, 50 percent when the beneficiary is twenty-five years of age, and so on. This arrangement provides a reasonable method of passing on your estate, minimizes the likelihood of frivolous waste, and makes it possible for the estate assets to continue to grow.

Such a course of action may seem callous and arbitrary, but you must remember that you worked hard to acquire your property and so want it to be put to the best possible use.

We have seen cases in which giving full control of substantial sums to a young person did more harm than good. The use of a partial payment raises the question of whether your children, when they receive a portion of your property at a set age, will waste the assets and, when they receive the next portion, do so again. It is to be hoped that they will learn by experience and be able to handle future installments with more skill and better judgment.

There are other possible arrangements. You can (1) plan for payments from the trust to be related to the needs of the recipient: for example, the beneficiary will receive more money at the start of his career, when earnings are low; or (2) set up a trust whereby the beneficiary receives all income but is not permitted to touch the principal. If the estate is large, this plan can have considerable merit.

In each case, what you decide to do should depend on the individual beneficiary and the assets involved. The beauty of the trust is that you get to write your own family financial plan.

With an income-only trust, you may create psychological problems by overprotecting the beneficiary. The heir may become dependent on the trust income and thus, ultimately, be harmed rather than aided. One of the factors motivating us to work, to create, and to provide for ourselves and our families is the uncertainty of tomorrow. Eliminate this uncertainty and you remove a valuable psychological prod. It may be true that most people continue to work after receiving an inheritance, but the impact of a large sum of money should be considered before the trust papers are completed.

From our experience, we do not believe that the distribution of any estate to a young person should be delayed beyond the thirty-fifth birthday except in special circumstances, as with a severely handicapped child or in a case involving such large sums that estate tax savings may make delay the most economical means of conserving wealth from one generation to the next. If the person is unable to handle an inheritance at the age of thirty-five, the chances are that he never will.

It avoids probate and guardianship. Through the device of a guardianship, a legal parent is provided for an individual who is incapable of managing his affairs because he is too young or lacks the requisite mental capacity. Usually, a guardian is appointed by the probate court in the county in which the ward (the individual being cared for) lives.

There are two types of guardianship:

1. *Guardian of the person.* A guardian of the person concerns himself with the ward's housing, food, clothing, medical bills, schooling, and other necessities. This type of guardian is usually a relative or family friend who knows the child and, presumably, has the ward's love and respect.
2. *Guardian of the estate.* This expression refers to an individual or a corporation, such as a bank, appointed to control and manage the ward's estate and property for the benefit of the ward. When the guardian is not a professional, the court may require the purchase of a bond to cover faithful performance. By means of such an insurance agreement, a guarantee is obtained against any possible financial loss caused by the default of the guardian. The court retains jurisdiction over administration, receives annual reports of actions and expenditures, and in some cases, must approve large distributions or decisions involving significant outlays.

The costs of providing for the guardianship of an estate can be high. The annual cost of a fidelity bond can be as much as one half of one percent of the value of the property being administered, and usually there will also be legal and guardian fees.

Guardianships of minors terminate when the legal age is attained. In many states this means eighteen, which most would agree is not the best time to take on the responsibility of a substantial inheritance.

Generally, the same person assumes both guardianship roles. With large estates, however, it may be wise to divide the responsibilities.

A trust can eliminate the need for the guardian of the estate, since property in trust is not subject to the probate process. It is set up for the heirs and distributed by the trustee in accordance with the terms of the trust agreement.

It provides a flexible means of administration and accommodation to change. The future may be unknowable, but the primary objective of estate planning, especially as concerns preparation of wills, is to prepare for problems that may occur one day. Here are typical questions we have encountered from clients:

- How much of his inheritance should my son spend for care and support?
- Should the trustee give him money to buy a new automobile or power boat?
- Should an artistically gifted daughter have funds to study abroad? And if she marries, how can I be sure that her funds from me will not be used improvidently by her husband?
- Should arrangements be made to provide my son with money with which to start a business or profession?
- How should the costs of postgraduate education be handled?
- What if my daughter wants to delay a career choice by attending graduate school?

It's hard to answer such queries as these correctly at any time, but it is even more difficult to do so before the situations arise, when you are making out your will. These decisions are important because, by law, after your death your last wishes must be carried out by your executor exactly as the terms of your will provide, no matter how conditions may have changed between then and the time of your signature.

Here again, the best answer, for many people asking such questions, is to create a trust. This arrangement transfers the decisionmaking power to a trustee and thus delays the need for a detailed solution until the problem arises.

The flexibility of the trust allows the trustee to make choices on the basis of the situation at the time, yet still work within the broad guidelines set forth in the trust agreement.

This ability to change is especially important with investments. Trustees need to be able to shift securities that will produce the best results for the trust. In the past, many trusts restricted investments—

to railroad bonds in the 1920s and to anything but real estate and common stocks in the late 1930s as the result of Depression bankruptcies. Such restrictions hampered trustees, resulting in decreased financial returns and lower appreciation, because following World War II there was a meteoric rise in common stocks that provided considerable protection against the erosion of inflation. In creating a trust, therefore, the best rule is to provide flexible investment powers and let the trustee adapt to take advantage of the best and safest opportunities.

It provides professional managers and advisers. There are three ways to get professional management when creating a trust: directly, by appointing a bank or trust company as trustee; indirectly, by empowering an individual trustee to retain advisers; or by a combination of both methods.

Many people typically say when thinking of arranging for a trustee: "I want somebody with a heart—somebody who will take care of my family." They fear that the professional will be impersonal and cold-hearted, that a trust officer will not be able to give the widow and children the sympathy and understanding they want and may need.

Although such fears are sometimes justified, we have found, through long experience, that usually the mark of a competent trust officer is his ability to help beneficiaries. Most of the men and women holding the position of trustee enjoy their work and become genuinely concerned with the personal problems of the beneficiaries. There is, of course, a limit to the time and effort they can give. If you feel that it is important for the trustee to have a personal involvement with your family, consider naming a cotrustee—perhaps your spouse, son, sister-in-law, or cousin—to work with the professional.

It saves on taxes. This advantage is explained in detail later, but broadly speaking, trusts can reduce or even eliminate taxes by:

1. *Dividing income among beneficiaries.* Income taxes are computed on a graduated scale: the more income, the higher the tax rate. By spreading the available income among two or more taxpayers, the tax is often lessened. In other words, "sprinkling" lowers the tax bracket and, thus, the tax.
2. *Withholding ownership rights.* A trust may be created so that the beneficiary, say a spouse, is not considered the "owner" of

the property in the trust. The beneficiary may receive all income and even some part of the principal if she needs it to maintain her standard of living. At her death, the property will not be taxed because, in tax and trust law terms, she is not considered the "owner." This is one of the most important features of a properly drawn trust and is responsible for millions of dollars of estate tax savings every year. More will be said about this particular feature of trusts in Chapter 6.

3. *Transferring income tax burdens.* Trusts can shift the obligation to pay taxes on property income from a high tax bracket person to a person or persons in lower tax brackets. This can be done on a permanent basis with a gift in trust or on a temporary basis with a "short-term" trust.

TYPES OF TRUSTS

Each of the many possible types of trusts can be described in terms of its suitability for a specific situation. Keep in mind that a trust is affected by tax codes and other laws which are complex, and therefore it should be drawn by an experienced attorney after careful consideration of the possible contingencies. In broad terms, trusts can be categorized in the following ways:

Trusts under will (testamentary trusts). According to this most common method of establishing trusts, the will provides that at death, all or a portion of the estate will be administered by a trustee, who will make distributions to certain individuals or organizations. Such a trust assures that your wishes will be carried out and that your beneficiaries will be treated properly. Usually, this type of trust also results in tax savings.

Example: Mr. Lewis has an estate of $300,000. His seventy-year-old wife has little knowledge of finance and tends to be a spendthrift. In his will, Mr. Lewis sets up a trust whereby his widow will be assured of $30,000 annually. The trustee bank is directed to pay her $2,500 each month. At a 6 percent annual return, this nest egg will last sixteen years; at 7 percent, eighteen years; at 8 percent, twenty-one years, and so on. If the trust yields an 8 percent return in the first year, the trust will earn $24,000. Therefore, the annual payment of $30,000 will deplete the principal or corpus of the trust by $6,000, and so on. And at 10 percent—not an unusual situation these days—no encroachment on principal will be necessary.

When children are involved, trusts under will can be flexible and set up to meet changing conditions. Typically, a *sprinkling trust* permits the trustee to distribute income and principal according to the specific needs of each of the beneficiaries.

Example: Mr. McCormick has three children: a son finishing dental college, a daughter married to a missionary, and a second son, who has recurrent health problems. The father wants to help each child but recognizes that the financial requirements of each may vary each year. He establishes a sprinkling trust so that the trustee has full power to allocate the $10,000 annual income according to the needs of the children. Here's how such a trust might work:

Year 1 The oldest son receives $6,000 to help him start his practice. The others get $2,000 each.

Year 2 The daughter, back home from abroad, is building a house, so she gets $5,000 and the balance is split between the two sons.

Year 3 The younger son becomes ill, so he receives $6,000, while $2,000 goes to each of the other children.

This example demonstrates how properly drawn trusts can be flexible and permit the trustee to provide humane as well as financial protection.

Inter vivos trusts. These "among living" trusts enable specific property to be administered and distributed during the lifetime of the creator. They are popular and widely used because: (1) property held in a living trust is not subject to the formalities of probate; (2) professional management can be designated for special investments such as real estate; (3) if it's irrevocable (cannot be terminated), income taxes can be saved by shifting income from the trustor, who is in a high tax bracket, to the beneficiary, who pays taxes at a lower rate; and (4) privacy of family finances can be maintained by avoiding probate.

Life insurance trust. This is like a living trust except that its only assets are insurance policies and, thus, during the trustor's lifetime there is no management responsibility. The trust is merely the beneficiary of the insurance. When the insured dies, the death proceeds will be paid to the trust, not an individual.

Usually, the insured person continues to pay the premiums and the trust lies dormant until he dies. But it is also possible to fund such a trust—to set up assets whose income is used to pay the premiums.

Most such trusts are revocable. During his lifetime, the insured retains all rights to the insurance and can cancel or borrow against the cash value of the policies. But irrevocable life insurance trusts are also possible and in special situations make sound estate planning sense!

A life insurance trust is useful for young professionals such as physicians, dentists, and lawyers, who, in their early careers, are unable to accumulate large assets directly or through personal retirement and profit-sharing plans. Frequently, they carry substantial life insurance in order to create a sizable estate quickly, thus protecting their young families from the loss of their income-producing ability.

Another advantage is that a life insurance trust will not be subject to probate, so there will be no delays and, except in rare cases, neither the proceeds nor the income will be subject to creditors' claims.

Gifts in trust. This type of trust enables you to give property when you are not sure of the recipient's ability to manage the assets, as with grandchildren or older relatives. It provides a convenient way to help others and also to avoid estate taxes on property that has appreciated between the date of the gift and the donor's death.

With such a trust, there is some measure of control and discretion in the use of the funds because the property is held in trust and administered by a designated trustee for the benefit of the recipient(s).

Gift trusts are often used by older people planning ways to reduce their future tax liabilities and, at the same time, to provide current financial aid to grandchildren for educational expenses, or to a charitable institution for special programs or continuing financial support.

Charitable trusts. Usually, these are family foundations, designed to make gifts to charitable institutions for the purpose of creating a memorial for the donors, their loved ones, or their families. In many cases, the trusts are set up when the wealthy individual is dissatisfied with the methods by which the charities administer or distribute funds or discovers a particular charitable cause that is unfunded.

Once they are established, they must be maintained, must make annual contributions, and must file voluminous reports—so it's not advisable to consider creating such funds unless substantial sums are involved.

The concept of charitable gifts is excellent and praiseworthy. Moreover, under present tax laws, gifts to charitable institutions which meet IRS qualifications are income tax deductible. But before you take action, make sure that the recipient agency is well run and will use your gift wisely.

If you want to make a sizable donation to a hospital, university, or social agency, check the capabilities and management of the potential recipient and consult an experienced attorney. In most cases, you will find that the charitable organization has the resources, background, and personnel to handle money more effectively than a trustee who is inexperienced in this specialized area.

From the charity's viewpoint, cash is usually most welcome, but for the donor, this seldom provides the greatest tax benefits. Usually, it is most advantageous to give property which has appreciated in value. The cost will be low and the tax deduction will be based on the current market value.

On the other hand, such gifts—often real estate or shares of a closely held corporation—tend to be illiquid. Once they become the property of the institution, they can be sold without the approval or knowledge of the donor.

Charitable remainder trust. This is an arrangement which will give you an immediate income tax deduction for your charitable contribution, will help to lower your estate taxes, and can provide income for you while the property is in trust. You establish a trust and arrange for the charity to get the money or property at some future date, usually at your death.

The amount you can deduct is based on IRS tables which consider your age, the value of the property, and the income from the trust. Generally, the older you are when you set up such a trust, the greater your deduction will be. But the IRS limits the deductions for gifts to public charities to 50 percent of your adjusted gross income when the gift is cash; to 30 percent (in most cases) when the donation involves appreciated securities. If the annual deductions exceed these limits, you can carry forward the excess for five years. A charitable remainder trust can also be established at your death for the benefit of another person—say your spouse—with the remainder of the trust to go to charity at the beneficiary's death.

These trusts require precise drafting, so always consult a tax-wise attorney. And make certain that the recipient is an organization for which gifts are deductible under IRS standards.

Revocable and irrevocable trusts. All trusts fall into one or the other of these categories, each of which has its advantages and disadvantages.

A person establishing a revocable trust retains the right to revoke it at any time. This type of trust may be used when the trustor is not sure how well the trust will be administered or how long he may want it to exist.

Example: Dr. Grass, a widower, has accumulated $500,000. He wants to leave his estate to his children, some of whom are still minors, but he is not convinced that a professional trustee will make the most rewarding investments or provide the personal empathy that he feels his children will need. Therefore, he establishes a revocable trust and names a bank as trustee.

After two years, he decides that the bank does not suit his wishes and revokes the trust. If Dr. Grass should die while the trust is in effect, these assets will be included in his taxable estate and thus subject to taxation.

With a revocable trust, you can keep adding to the assets as long as you live. Or if you suffer financial reverses, you can withdraw some assets from it.

An irrevocable trust is the opposite. A person establishing this type of trust loses the right to terminate the agreement, cannot receive any income, cannot use the assets as collateral for a loan or in any way exercise control of the trust. If the creator of an irrevocable trust retains any of these types of benefits in the trust assets, the IRS will consider the trust revocable and a part of the creator's taxable estate.

At his death, if three years have passed since the transfer without any retained rights, the property will not be considered a part of his estate, but the value of the trust at the date of the gift will be included in the estate for purposes of calculating the unified federal tax credit.

Irrevocable trusts have two advantages: (1) the income from the trust assets are not taxable to the trustor; (2) the appreciation, over the years, will not be taken into account for estate taxes as long as the donor survives for three years after transferring the assets to the trust.

Short-term trusts. Many trusts are structured to pass on property, but short-term trusts are created primarily to avoid income taxes. They transfer income from someone with a high tax rate to someone else, in a much lower tax bracket. In theory, short-term trusts are advantageous; in practice, they are suitable only in a limited number of situations.

By law, a short-term trust has a minimum life of ten years or the lifetime of the individual for whose benefit the trust will operate. While the property is in trust, all its income goes to the beneficiary. On termination, the principal reverts to the original donor.

Use short-term trusts cautiously. Remember that you must be ready to accept loss of control over your property for a long time and also be willing to have all its income go to someone else.

In some situations, this kind of arrangement can be dangerous—for example, when the transferred assets are highly specialized, such as real estate, which requires personal attention, or stock representing the controlling interest in a corporation. Once the trust is established, there's nothing the donor can do about it!

Watch the tax angle. All distributed income is taxable to the beneficiary at regular income tax rates. If the beneficiary, often a child or needy relative, receives unexpected income, his tax bracket will be so high that there will no longer be any tax advantage.

Don't get carried away by the idea of tax avoidance. Ten years is a long time, during which many changes can take place, in your own fortunes and in those of the people you seek to help.

Generally, short-term trusts are suitable for high-income families who, temporarily, can afford to spare some or all of their investment income but want to get back both the capital gains and earning power of the property.

Specifically, short-term trusts are often used for:

Supporting an aged parent. Mr. O'Toole, who is in the 50 percent tax bracket, contributes $3,200 to the support of his eighty-year-old mother. Because of taxes, he has to earn $6,400 to provide this sum.

He has $40,000 in 8 percent bonds that yield $3,200 annually. He uses them to set up a short-term trust that will continue for ten years or as long as his mother lives.

This arrangement assures the needed income, and Mr. O'Toole will pay less in taxes because his reportable income will be lower. At his mother's death, he will get back the $40,000—or more, if the property has appreciated in value.

College trust. Mr. Ross has an eight-year-old daughter, who, he expects, will start college in ten years. His taxable income is $37,500, so he's in the 45 percent tax bracket. A short-term trust of $15,000 will provide his daughter with $1,200 a year. Mr. Ross will pay the income taxes. Through reinvestment of all income and appreciation, the trust will grow so that when the daughter is eighteen, she will have enough money to pay for most of the tuition costs and, perhaps, some expenses too.

Minor children. Lawyer Lyon has four children, all under twelve years of age. His net income, before exemptions, is $37,000, of which $3,000 represents interest on $60,000 worth of government bonds. He pays a tax of $8,870, so he nets $28,310.

He can save on taxes by setting up four separate trusts, in each of which he places $15,000 in bonds. Each child will then receive $750 of income, tax free, and Mr. Lyon gets annual tax savings of $1,875.

As the children grow older and start earning money on their own, they may have to pay taxes, probably at a low 14 percent rate.*

Salesman Smith has a twelve-year-old son who wants to be a lawyer and estimates that, at a minimum, the costs of graduate school will be $30,000. In the 45 percent tax bracket, he must tie up $36,000, at an 8 percent annual return, to provide this money.

Mr. Smith sets up a short-term trust with $19,800. At 8 percent, this will compound to the needed sum. Better yet, the father will have an extra $750 in spendable annual income due to lower taxes.

These examples show how tax savings can be achieved with short-term trusts. If you feel financially secure enough to get along without substantial funds for ten years, short-term trusts can be useful. But do not place more value on the tax benefits than on personal or family needs.

---

*CAUTION: If funds in a trust are used to satisfy the legal support obligations of the creator of the trust (in some states, this includes college education), the trust will be taxed to the donor.

Remember Trusts can:

1. Continue beyond your lifetime.
2. Avoid probate.
3. Keep your financial affairs private.
4. Provide professional management.
5. Avoid taxes.
6. Provide a flexible means of administering investments over a period of changing conditions.

6

Estate and inheritance taxes

- **The value of a decedent's property is subject to federal estate tax laws**
- **Many states also levy a death tax**
- **These taxes can often be substantially reduced by the proper use of trusts**

In estate planning, it is essential to consider the taxes that will be imposed following the death of persons with property. Once you establish your financial objectives and assess your wealth, you need expert assistance to determine how to keep the maximum amount of your estate for your heirs by minimizing inheritance and estate taxes.

The first inheritance tax of the U.S. government was enacted in 1797, but was repealed in 1802. For the next century, the federal estate tax was on and off by turns—revived to help finance wars and repealed with peace. The tax was imposed during the Civil War, repealed in 1870, adopted again in the Spanish-American War, dropped in 1902. In 1916, the federal estate tax as we know it today was established. Over the years, there have been frequent revisions, with dramatic changes in 1976.

In addition to the federal estate tax, most states have enacted a death tax, on either the inheritance or the estate. Some of these levies date back to the early 1800s. These terms, *inheritance tax* and *estate tax,* have different meanings. An inheritance tax is assessed against the person who receives the property after the death of someone. Normally, this levy is determined by the total amount inherited and the relationship of the beneficiary to the deceased—for example, a son of a decedent would pay taxes at a lower rate than would a cousin of a decedent. An estate tax is imposed on the entire estate and does not necessarily look to the relationship between the heirs and the deceased. Generally, except when the beneficiary is the spouse of the deceased, the levy is the same no matter who receives the property.

When states have both taxes, the estate tax would be levied only

49

rarely. Usually, the purpose of such a tax is to take advantage of the credit allowed against the federal estate tax for state inheritance taxes where the state taxes are not high enough to use up all the allowable federal credit. As you add to your assets, review the potential tax liabilities with your attorney and be ready to make changes in your estate plan to reduce taxes and meet requirements of new legislation and regulations.

Time is an important consideration in the payment of estate and inheritance taxes. The federal tax is due nine months after the date of death, and most states require payment at about the same time or a few months thereafter. However, it is possible to get extensions for both levies. Postponement of payment can be important when the estate is complicated or when substantial property is involved, because to meet tax deadlines, some properties may have to be sold at below-value prices.

For all intents and purposes, all property owned by the decedent at death is subject to tax at its value on the date of death, not on what may have been paid for it when acquired by the decedent. There is no life insurance exemption as far as the federal government is concerned, and when there are state exemptions, they are generally limited to certain amounts, depending on the relationship between the insured and the beneficiary.

The 1976 Federal Tax Reform Act enhanced provisions which allow for the delay in the payment of estate taxes. Under some circumstances, tax payments may be suspended for five years after death and then paid over the succeeding ten-year period. The rate of interest in such cases is also quite favorable.

In all matters concerning death taxes, consult your lawyer. The federal estate tax return is a sixteen-page document available without charge from the U.S. Treasury Department. The 1976 changes in the laws are so new that not even tax experts or IRS agents really understand all their implications and provisions. Already, there are volumes of rules, regulations, and reports that interpret and give advice on the new law.

At the present time, these are the highlights of the federal law on the taxation of estates.

1. There's an option to value property at the date of death or within six months from that date. If the estate holds assets

which were declining in value at the owner's death, this option allows the estate to avoid some of the sting by permitting the estate tax to be based on the lower value six months after death.

However, the law does state that all assets must be appraised at the same time. You cannot choose different dates for different assets.

2. Deductions from the gross value of the estate are permitted for such expenses as the funeral, administration, debts, mortgages, and liens against the property. What is left after these deductions is the net value, or "adjusted gross estate," which forms the basis for tax calculations.

3. If the deceased was survived by a spouse, the estate is allowed a further deduction, called the "marital deduction." This consists of $250,000 or one half of the adjusted gross estate—whichever is greater.

To qualify for this important saving, the manner in which the surviving spouse receives the property is important. The survivor must be given certain minimum rights to the property: rights to all income, and the power at death to dispose of the inheritance to whomever he or she wants. Property given outright or in joint tenancy qualifies.

4. No federal estate tax return need be filed unless the total gross estate (before allowable deductions) is greater than the unified tax credit: in 1980, $161,000, rising to $175,000 in 1981.

These filing requirements assume that no part of any specific exemption or unified credit is used up by means of gifts made by the decedent after September 8, 1976.

5. States may require a complete accounting regardless of the size of the estate. It's not unusual for a state inheritance or estate tax to be imposed even though no federal estate tax is due.

THE 1976 FEDERAL TAX REFORM ACT*

This revolutionary law, enacted in 1976, made important changes in taxation of estates by (1) unifying estate and gift taxes; (2) establishing a higher minimum marital deduction, and as a result, (3) drastically cutting taxes on smaller estates.

*As corrected by the Technical Corrections part of the Revenue Act of 1978.

There are no longer separate tax schedules for gifts and estates. The old provision, exempting $30,000 in lifetime gifts, has been eliminated in favor of a unified tax credit which increases from $34,000 in 1978 to $47,000 in 1981 and thereafter. Normally, an estate tax return does not have to be filed until the gross estate (before allowable deductions, as explained earlier) is greater than the unified tax credit.

Year of death	Unified tax credit	Taxable estate†
1978	$34,000	$134,000
1979	38,000	147,333
1980	42,500	161,563
1981 and on	47,000	175,625

†Size of taxable estate before tax is due

You are still allowed to make gifts to any one person, without tax or report, to a maximum of $3,000 a year. Above that limit, gifts made within three years of death are automatically included in the donor's gross estate, and if a gift tax has been paid, it is also includable in the gross estate.

Gifts by spouses to a third party can total $6,000 in any one year without incurring any tax. However, gift tax returns would have to be filed signifying a spouse's consent.

The credit is a lifetime one, so that if, through the years, taxable gifts are made and some of the unified credit is used, only the remainder, if any, is available to reduce the estate tax.

It still pays to make gifts of property that are likely to appreciate in value, because the gain is not taxable. But generally, there are no longer tax incentives for older people to give away assets on which substantial gains have been achieved. There are exceptions for gifts within a family. For example, when you give to a spouse, the first $100,000, under the federal law, is fully deductible; the next $100,000 is fully taxable; and above $200,000, half of the gifts are subject to tax.

The new law as it applies to gifts is tricky. Be sure to consult with a knowledgeable lawyer *before* making any substantial gifts.

For most people, the most important change in the law was in the marital deduction, which was raised to $250,000 or one half of the adjusted gross estate, whichever is greater.

Example: A man dies in 1980 with an estate of $400,000 after settlement expenses. No taxable gifts have been made. After the marital deduction of $250,000, the taxable estate is $150,000, on which the federal tax is $38,800. From this is deducted the unified credit of $42,500 and the state death tax credit of $400, so the net federal estate tax is zero.

If the man dies in 1981, he can pass on an estate of $425,625 without a federal estate tax. By that time, the basic $250,000 marital deduction would be supplemented by a $47,000 unified tax credit sufficient to allow the remaining $175,625 to pass tax free.

Generation-skipping transfers. The new law seeks to discourage the establishment of long-term trusts which pass property from generation to generation with little or no estate tax. However, the law does allow an exclusion from the generation-skipping transfer tax by excluding from the amount subject to tax the sum of $250,000 for each child of the decedent who has a child. This sum is a total, regardless of how many grandchildren may be involved. For example: A dies survived by son B, who has three children, and daughter C, who has no children. A's estate would be entitled to a $250,000 generation-skipping transfer exclusion. If C had one or more children, the amount would be $500,000.

There are special provisions which "grandfather in" until January 1, 1982, wills and revocable trusts with generation-skipping features that were in existence on or before June 11, 1976, so be cautious about altering such instruments.

The effect of these new provisions can be avoided somewhat by establishing a series of trusts for each separate generation.

Carry-over basis. The 1976 Tax Reform Act made changes in the tax basis value of inherited property in the hands of heirs. Previously, for purposes of federal estate tax, securities, real estate, and similar property were valued at their worth at the date of death of the owner or at the alternate date, six months later, *regardless of the original cost.* This same date-of-death worth was used by heirs in calculating their costs for tax purposes. As a result of this arrangement, many older people held property until they died in order not to pay income taxes on appreciation that would be realized if they sold at a profit.

The new law changed the rule so that those who inherited property acquired the deceased person's cost.

This meant that heirs faced the prospect of substantially increased taxes: first, estate taxes paid on date-of-death values of inherited property; later, when that property was sold, additional taxes, this time income taxes, on the difference between the decedent's tax basis (usually purchase cost) and value at the time of the sale. From the time of its passage in 1976 through 1979, there was much discussion by tax specialists, congressmen, and probate lawyers. Prodigious record-keeping would be imposed and a substantial increase in taxes loomed. Nightmare situations existed. A moratorium on implementation of the new law went into effect for the period 1977 through 1979, and finally, on *March* 2, 1980 it was repealed. The result of all this is that the law remains the same: a person inheriting property receives a stepped-up basis for capital gains purposes—the value of the property at the date of death (or six months later if the alternative valuation method is used) of the one from whom the property is inherited.

The 1976 Tax Reform Act has other important aspects, such as special real estate valuation relief for farmers and owners of closely held businesses, and extension of time to pay estate taxes; a fractional-interest rule for taxation of jointly owned property; orphans exclusion; new rules regarding the taxability of retirement benefits, and many other provisions.

Qualifying for these special reliefs may prove difficult and not many of the new measures will apply to your personal or family situations. Yet everyone who has substantial property should retain a knowledgeable attorney and review his estate plan in light of this new law.

CUTTING TAXES ON THE DEATH OF THE SURVIVING SPOUSE

The estate of one spouse may be subject to two tax bites in a relatively short span of time—once at the death of the first to die and then again at the death of the survivor. Tax-wise attorneys can significantly reduce this problem through the use of a two-trust arrangement.

Example: Mrs. Wilson is left $400,000 outright by her husband, who dies in 1981. She will pay no federal tax, but if she does not remarry, the federal tax on her estate could be as much as $68,000.

The estate taxes could be reduced or avoided by the creation of two trusts:

1. *Trust A,* also known as a "marital trust" or "wife's trust," would be for the sole benefit of Mrs. Wilson and would cover $225,000 of her assets.
2. *Trust B,* a "family trust," would take care of the remaining $175,000 in assets.

Under Trust A, Mrs. Wilson would receive at least the income of the estate during her lifetime and, usually, portions of the principal. Lawyers use language such as: "My wife may have as much principal as is needed for her care, maintenance, and support, including reasonable luxuries." Translated, this means that she should be allowed to have what she needs to maintain the standard of living to which she is accustomed. She must also have the power to dispose of Trust A to whomever she wants at her death. There is no need that the A part of $225,000 be in trust. It could go outright to Mrs. Wilson at Mr. Wilson's death.

Under Trust B, the widow usually receives the income for her life, and additional principal which may be necessary for her support (after the principal in Trust A has been exhausted). At her death the remaining principal in Trust B (and the remaining principal in Trust A if she has not otherwise exercised her power) will usually go the couple's children.

None of the assets in Trust B will become part of Mrs. Wilson's taxable estate, because she did not have unlimited use of the property. By means of Trust B, the tax, at Mrs. Wilson's death, is reduced to $14,000, for a saving of $54,000. Generally, administration of such trusts is best accomplished by a third party.

STATE DEATH TAXES

Don't forget that you may have to pay state death and gift taxes (especially when substantial assets are involved) even if, in some cases, you don't have to pay a federal estate or gift tax.

State death taxes on large estates will average one third to one half the taxes of the federal government. Not all states have gift taxes, but those that do tax major gifts at a rate that is approximately 20 percent of the federal gift tax rate.

REVIEW BY THE IRS

All federal estate tax returns are audited by the Internal Revenue Service. Usually the depth of the review is related to the size and complexity of the estate. The simplest review is a desk audit made at the local IRS office without the presence of a representative of the executor. Large estates, or estates belonging to persons who over the years have reported little income, are given more detailed scrutiny.

Note: Property received by inheritance is not subject to any income tax—federal, state, or municipal. Nor need the money or property you inherit be reported on your annual personal income tax return. However, there *are* taxes on the income or appreciation realized on such property.

According to a legal aphorism, there are two federal estate taxes: one for people who have planned their estate, the other for those who have failed to plan properly. There can be vast differences between the two levies.

Even if you have a modest estate, you will find it worth your while to start financial planning early in life. Planning can save money on taxes while you live and after you die. You will find the small cost of professional counsel to be far more than repaid in tax savings, plus added security and happiness for your loved ones.

Remember

1. The 1976 Tax Reform Act substantially changed the manner and amount of death levies—especially on estates under $500,-000.
2. If your estate plan has not been reviewed by an estate planning attorney since 1976, you should seek review and advice immediately.
3. If you are married, your attorney will probably suggest the use of tax-saving trust(s) in your plan; one will be subject to tax at your death and the other at the death of your spouse.
4. Without this arrangement, your estate may pay substantially increased taxes and your children will receive less than they would through proper planning.

Table 1 COMPUTATION OF FEDERAL TAX ON ESTATES

DEATH IN 1981 (NO GIFTS OVER $3,000 TO ANY SINGLE DONEE AFTER SEPTEMBER 8, 1976)

Value of gross estate		$660,000
Deductions for debts, funeral expenses, administration	$60,000	
Adjusted gross estate		600,000
Marital deduction	300,000	
Net taxable estate		300,000
Tax before unified credit		87,800
Unified credit		47,000
Federal tax before state credit		40,800
Less credit for state death taxes		(3,600)
Net federal estate tax		$37,200

7

Estate planning

Estate planning refers to the thoughtful arrangement of one's affairs and the disposition of one's property with the assistance of technical experts. It has as its basic purposes to meet an individual's objectives in life and to ensure attainment of specific goals for beneficiaries after the planner's death.

It is not a do-it-yourself, once-over-lightly process. A successful estate plan involves a thorough review of one's current assets and future prospects, and requires the expertise of a skilled attorney as well as, often, an insurance agent, a trust officer, and an accountant. It is feasible to start your own estate planning, but without proper counsel, your hopes may be frustrated and your beneficiaries may have to face seemingly endless difficulties.

Here are the basic steps you can take to set yourself on the right path for effective estate planning.

Take inventory. List *all* your assets: your home, furniture, automobile, jewelry, savings and checking accounts, your share in employee benefit plans, securities, real estate, life insurance, and anything else of value. A full, accurate inventory will give you an idea of what should be done, what has to be accomplished in the future, and how you should distribute your estate among your family and loved ones. It will also help your attorney and other advisers to implement your wishes wisely, with a view to minimum tax liability and the greatest protection now and in the future.

Insofar as possible, the inventories should be compiled in cooperation with your spouse and—when they are old enough—your children.

Since the legal documents needed to set up your plan rarely men-tion specific assets or their values, it's satisfactory to approximate the total worth. It is, however, of paramount importance to determine the title to each item, the date of its acquisition, and the cost at that time. Questions to be asked in the process of taking inventory include:

- Is your real estate held in joint tenancy? If so, by whom?
- Are securities held in joint tenancy? If so, by whom?
- Are assets held in your name only?
- Who is the beneficiary of your life insurance and does the beneficiary receive the death proceeds outright or in installments?
- Provisions of any divorce decrees?
- Provisions of buy/sell or other business agreements/stock options?

Accuracy is important in answering such questions, so examine each bankbook, stock certificate, insurance policy, real estate deed, and any other item very carefully. Unless you have acquired considerable wealth, there's no need to hire an appraiser, but for tax purposes it's a good idea to have two figures for real estate and securities: *the date of their acquisition* and *their value at that time.*

The Net Worth Work Sheet on pages 62–63 should assist you in taking an initial inventory and then updating it annually. The items listed in the outline will, of course, vary from individual to individual.

After adding all your assets and subtracting all your liabilities, you will get your net worth: the net amount of your estate at the time of inventory.

Keep everything up to date annually. A business has a financial statement prepared yearly—so should you.

Keep your projections flexible. If you or anyone else in your family stands to inherit property, benefit from a trust fund, or gain other assets, add the likely sum to the proper column with an asterisk (*). This is to indicate that you are not including such possibilities of wealth in your primary calculations, but will consider them in determining your estate plan.

Spell out your objectives. Be clear about your objectives in order to provide the framework needed by your advisers. As you plan your estate, focus on what might happen in the event of your death. What provision do you want to make for your spouse? For the children?

Think of what would happen if there were a disaster which took the lives of both parents or even one parent and the children?

Keep in mind that your will and your estate will survive you. Their effects will be felt by your spouse, your children, and, possibly, your grandchildren throughout their lifetimes. A will or estate plan that may engender bitterness runs counter to the objectives of sound estate planning, which is to add happiness and economic security for your loved ones' future prospects.

Make your plan for the long term. Even if you feel that each child in the family is different—let's say one of them is a spendthrift—think carefully before you make any special provisions. Treating one child differently may do him more harm than good, not only in relation to his happiness (how he remembers you and regards your attitude toward him), but also because it may influence his future ability to handle property.

Responsible management of money and property is difficult to learn without actual experience. Years ago, well-to-do fathers customarily established lifetime provisions for their daughters. The father, not quite certain that a daughter would make a "good" marriage, thus ensured continuing support for her. Or a father who was worried that his son would gamble might limit him to the income from his inheritance. However, such practices are seldom relevant to today's changed circumstances and so are rarely used.

Common sense should play the biggest role in setting your objectives. For example, you should be aware that if your wife survives you and your children are minors, the value of your estate will probably undergo a strain, especially with ever rising costs of college and other post–high school training. Furthermore, if the children are very young, they will need the mother's guidance, so that it may be difficult for her to undertake a career.If she does work, there will be the extra expenses of day care for the children.

The number one concern of most married men is their wives. Notwithstanding ERA and changing womens' roles in society, husbands feel a continuing responsibility for their wives and with good reason. The children will grow up and leave to get married and pursue their own careers. In many cases, however, the wife will find herself out of touch with the job market and, due to age and lack of employable skills, will have difficulty in securing adequately paid employment.

In most families, the husband undertakes the responsibility of trying to build and plan his estate to provide reasonable lifetime security for the woman who became his marriage partner. This does not mean that an estate plan should be for the wife's exclusive benefit. If the resources of the estate are substantial enough, some funds should also be made available to the children during their mother's lifetime.

Such provisions could be in the form of direct bequests or funds held in trust; the terms of the trust would depend upon the size of the estate and the needs and maturity of the children. There is no reason why assets should not be used to help children pay for postgraduate education, start a business, or acquire a homestead. So when you have provided adequate protection for your wife, consider in what ways your property can bring the greatest happiness to your children or grandchildren.

Set up the plan. Once you know your assets and have defined your objectives, the next step is to implement your plan. To do this, you will need to choose people who will now advise you further and explain to you how best to carry out your program.

At this point, you may be discouraged and you may fear that your estate is not large enough to do the job you have in mind. The single best solution for someone in this situation is life insurance. A good insurance agent can help you to bring your estate up to a point at which it will adequately support your widow and children while they are still dependents.

Life insurance comes in all sizes and shapes, but the basic purpose is "death" protection: to provide money at the death of the insured. Upon proof of the death of a policyholder, the insurance company pays a predetermined sum (the face value of the policy plus accumulations, if any, minus any outstanding loans) to the designated beneficiary or beneficiaries. This provides ready money to meet the financial needs of the heirs.

There are two general categories of life insurance:

1. *Straight life.* This kind of insurance builds cash values with the payment of premiums larger than needed to assure protection alone. Over the years, there is a slow, steady increase in the assets (cash value). This can be important in estate planning, because this money becomes the basis for borrowing or,

Table 2 NET WORTH WORK SHEET

ASSETS	Held in Own Name	Held Jointly	Comments
CASH AND EQUIVALENTS			
Checking accounts			
Saving accounts			
Life insurance			
Cash value			
Face value			
Beneficiary			
Equity in pension plan			
Debts owed to you			
Other			
POSSESSIONS			
Automobiles			
Appliances			
Furniture and equipment			
Recreation and hobby items			
Collections			
Furs, jewelry, etc.			
Other valuables			
REAL ESTATE			
Home			
Vacation cottage			
Other land or property			

Table 2   (continued)

A S S E T S *(continued)*	Held in Own Name	Held Jointly	Comments
INVESTMENTS			
Stocks and bonds			
Mutual fund shares			
Business interests			
Other			
Total Assets			
L I A B I L I T I E S			
Mortgage balance			
Current bills			
Charge accounts			
Credit card charges			
Installment loans			
Margin account			
Insurance loans			
Taxes due			
Pledges to charity			
Other			
Total Liabilities			
NET WORTH			

through dividends earned on the investment of these funds, reduces the annual carrying costs.

2. *Term life.* This insurance, which provides protection but builds no cash value, is strictly a death benefit. Generally, term life insurance is sold for a short period of time, five or ten years, and can then be renewed at a higher premium. One of its great advantages is that it can be used to create an "instant" estate when you are young and have not accumulated substantial wealth. As the children grow older and are able to earn money on their own, the amount of money needed for their support becomes smaller and you can afford to drop some of the term life coverage.

A cheaper form of protection is known as "decreasing term life insurance." This insurance is widely used with mortgages because its terms provide that the death payment decreases as the equity in the home increases—for example, a twenty-year mortgage of $70,000 would be balanced by a $70,000 decreasing term life policy. As the mortgage is amortized, the value of the insurance drops proportionately and disappears with the last mortgage payment.

Think of the role of your wife in handling the estate. One of the most frequently asked questions we have heard in helping plan an estate is: "How much freedom should be given my wife?"

In most cases, we answer, "Plenty." Many husbands fear leaving their wives in complete control of the property. They think that, especially if their wives become widows while still young and of marriageable age, they will be duped or conned. The fact is that most widows who lose any of their inheritance do so by error of omission rather than by commission. These ladies are cautious, often overly so. Sometimes a situation does arise in which a widow is beguiled by "brother Charley and his get-rich-quick schemes." However, the more typical widow is so chary about outside advice that she generally disregards all counsel, and that sometimes includes the advice of competent persons given responsibilities by her husband.

As a general rule, we advise that the wife take an active part in estate planning: in the inventory, in outlining objectives, and in the development of the will and the establishment of trusts. We also suggest that the husband give his widow considerable freedom in han-

dling the estate. And above all, make sure she understands and partici-
pates to the fullest in the estate planning.

The husband should concentrate on choosing competent advisers
and in planning to leave his property in such a way that, on his death,
these advisers automatically appear on the scene and are prepared to
help the widow and children.

Where both spouses work. The preceding portions of this chapter
have been devoted for the most part to situations where the male
member of the household has been the breadwinner.

In young America today, it is the exception, rather than the rule,
when the male is the sole breadwinner. Statistics show that today in
young marriage situations, nearly all wives work—and often it is many
years after marriage before children come along and sometimes
never. In fact, from time to time, there are situations where the female
of the marriage does better financially than the male.

From an estate planning viewpoint, this type of situation—until
children come along—does not present a great problem. If either
spouse dies, the other really has no problem of support. He or she has
already demonstrated this capability.

In marriages without children where both spouses work, the trend
today seems to be to "spend everything." They seem to forget that the
day may come along when they will have to live on only one salary.
Sometimes the best estate planning advice that can be given couples
of this type is financial advice. Pay yourself first. Put regular sums
away. So simple, yet so difficult.

Where there are children involved, it is always quite clear that the
parents want whatever there is, if both are deceased, to be used for
the care and maintenance of the children.

In marriages without children, the concern is what will happen to
whatever estate has been built up after both parties die. If the parties
have not carefully attended to details, it well could develop that one
side of the family would get everything.

For instance, say a young man, recently married and with no children, dies without a will, leaving everything to his wife, and within a
few days she, too, dies—perhaps the result of a common accident. In
most states, all the wealth they had accumulated, even if recently
given to the young man by his relatives, would pass to his surviving
wife, and on her death all her wealth would go to her side of the family.

This could produce a very unfair situation. The family of the first to die had a hand in creating the wealth of the parties, but because no planning had taken place, everything was left to the family of the last to die. With proper planning, all this could have been avoided.

ESTATE PLANNING FOR SINGLES

Obviously, unmarried persons should give careful thought to the planning of their estates. Although many single persons do not have dependents or persons who regularly receive support and financial assistance from them, they should have an interest in seeing that in the event of death, their estates are distributed to those persons and organizations they wish to benefit and with a minimum tax cost and administrative expense. While outright distribution from a simple will may be appropriate for parents, brothers, sisters, and recognized charities, the use of trusts should also be considered. An aged parent or a minor niece or nephew would make an excellent case for the use of a trust under will.

Older singles who do not have spouses or children to assist them with the administration of their financial affairs should consider the creation of an inter vivos trust, so that if their abilities to administer their financial affairs should diminish severely, their trustee will be ready to assume the tasks.

It has been our experience that most single persons with children, whether by divorce or by death of a spouse, are especially concerned about what will happen to the children if he or she dies. Accordingly, plans are made. The plan usually results in a trust arrangement for the children if they are minors.

There has been a great deal of recent publicity about unmarried persons who live together, sometimes sharing a homestead, oftentimes sharing expenses and income as well. Obviously, it is important from a legal point of view that these parties receive competent legal and tax advice. Generally speaking, most state laws do not recognize a common-law marital relationship. Thus, the surviving partner would receive no inheritance at law—i.e., in situations where the decedent died without a will. Unmarried persons who desire to leave their estates or a portion of their property to an unmarried partner should have a properly drawn will providing for such a distribution. Without this, the surviving partner would have to base his or her claim on some form of contract. If a written agreement does not exist, the survivor's chances of receiving anything are poor. This is a developing area of law and it is extremely important that persons who find themselves in these circumstances receive competent legal advice.

SECOND MARRIAGES

The number of divorced and widowed persons who remarry is substantial. From an estate planning point of view, their circumstances often differ from those marrying for the first time. In many cases, there are separate estates and separate families and sometimes minor children. The second marriage may present a conflict of motives: a desire to provide care for the surviving spouse but also to recognize the interests of children born of the prior marriage. Many enter the second marriage without giving thought to this serious topic, only to find themselves later in a legal predicament.

It is extremely important that one receive competent legal advice *before* undertaking the second marriage. It is probable that the lawyer dealing with such a case will recommend that the parties enter into a prenuptial or antenuptial agreement. Such an agreement will usually specify separate assets and estates and their separate intentions as to distribution on death. A well-drawn antenuptial agreement overrides state laws requiring distribution to surviving spouses.

There are several pitfalls in this area, among them:

1. Not recognizing the need for such an agreement until after the marriage. The enforceability of agreements entered after marriage is not clear in many states, and in fact such postnuptial agreements may be unenforceable. This underlines the importance of making the agreement prior to the second marriage ceremony.
2. Each party should consult his or her own attorney. There is a natural conflict of interest between parties entering into an antenuptial agreement and it is almost impossible for one attorney to properly represent both parties. The emotions of those contemplating marriage do not usually lend themselves to separate legal consultation—but this should be undertaken.

OWNERSHIP OF PROPERTY IN MORE THAN ONE STATE

We are a mobile society and more and more people are acquiring property, usually a vacation home, in a state other than their state of residence. Often this means that on the death of the owner there must be two parallel probate proceedings: one in the state of residence and the other in the state in which the property is located. This almost always adds to the total cost of probating the decedent's estate and thus should be avoided if practicable. This "extra" probate is sometimes referred to as an ancillary probate.

One of the best ways of avoiding a double probate is through the prudent use of joint tenancy where the owners are married to each other; or through the use of a partnership entity to hold title. On occasion, a revocable trust could even be used.

8

The role of the lawyer and estate planning aides

In estate planning, your lawyer is the key person. He is the "captain" of the team, which, depending on the scope of your assets, may include a trust officer, an insurance agent, an accountant, and an investment adviser.

Your lawyer, by training and tradition, should have one primary obligation—*to you, his client.* He strives to give each client the full benefit of his knowledge and experience; ideally, he will advise against something he feels is not in your best interest and carefully scrutinize all proposals and provide impartial counsel.

He is in the best position to make the required suggestions, to ask the required questions, and to render the required judgments, because his income and continued success as a professional depend on his having the proper expertise and having served only you, his client. The attorney who helps in planning your estate should have no incentive to spend or invest your money. His compensation should be set by a predetermined, though not necessarily fixed, fee arrangement, usually on an hourly basis.

Before discussing how to choose a lawyer, let's review the other people who can be helpful in estate planning. How important they might be to you will depend on the size of your estate, your family responsibilities, and what you wish to be done after your death. Some lawyers who are specialists in estate planning and probate sometimes resent and even oppose outside assistance, but we think this is an unjustified attitude. In more than forty years of joint experience, we have found that the majority of lawyers' "partners" in estate planning are concerned, helpful, and anxious to serve the best interests of their clients. Generally, there are four of them:

Trust officer. The executives of most trust companies conduct themselves in a professional manner and try to produce the best results for each client. Whether this is due to altruism or the desire to preserve the institution's reputation for integrity, thereby maintaining its competitive status, is of no practical importance. A professional trustee can render valuable service.

Life insurance agent. Whether you have a little or a lot of insurance, a life insurance agent should be involved in your estate planning. He does have a selfish motive in that his income depends upon the sale of insurance, but life insurance is nevertheless important to a family at all stages. It provides protection for a young family; it assures a balanced investment program during middle age; and it makes possible tax savings and security at retirement.

In recent years, no industry has done more to invoke professional standards and performance in its sales force than the life insurance industry. The designation CLU (Chartered Life Underwriter) is held only by those who have undergone extensive training in various aspects of estate planning and who have successfully passed a series of written examinations. We have found that most people with the CLU designation are competent, professional, and able to provide worthwhile advice.

Investment adviser. It often is advisable to have a firm or an individual as an investment adviser if your estate consists of a number of securities or business investments. If you prefer to handle your own money while you live, you should make arrangements for your estate representative to retain counsel. As outlined earlier, do not hesitate to designate an investment adviser to work with the bank or trust company responsible for handling your estate or trust.

Accountant. Many persons, especially those who are in business, rely greatly on the advice of their accountant. These advisers are often the best source of financial data in an estate planning case. An accountant who is a CPA (Certified Public Accountant) has received special training and experience and has passed a difficult qualifying examination.

CHOOSING YOUR LAWYER

Selecting an attorney to help you in estate planning is a serious and often a difficult task. The average person does not even know a lawyer. Occasionally, he is the guy next door who says "Hi" over the fence— or a high school classmate whose firm's office is next door to the bank. You have no way of knowing whether such an individual can draft a good plan or advise you properly.

Approval of advertising by lawyers is so recent that only a few attorneys have utilized this form of public information. In most cases, when you seek legal counsel, you must rely on recommendations and reputation.

One source for recommendations could be your insurance agent, especially if he works in the estate planning area. Keep in mind, however, that that does not necessarily mean he will be a good judge of legal competence.

You can also inquire at your bank. Most trust departments have estate planning divisions that work with local attorneys, and their experience in dealing with both customers and lawyers can be useful. Furthermore, some states and large cities have bar reference organizations with whom many qualified attorneys register; such an organization may provide a starting point for recommendations.

However you make your selection, check the individual and his firm carefully. You are hiring someone who will be intimately involved with your future—for many years, you hope. Usually, a family lawyer should be able to handle estate planning. That's one of the reasons for engaging a family lawyer in the first place. But when your property is large or diverse, you may need a specialist. He should then supplement, not replace, your family attorney.

A good family lawyer can give you and your loved ones peace of mind just by being available. He can save you dollars by preventing you from making a costly mistake. He can provide counsel during negotiations and litigation and support in family crises such as death.

Approach the selection of your lawyer as you would any business proposition. But most important, make sure he is working only for you and only in your best interests and those of your family. Set down the specific needs you have, and once you have narrowed down your list of candidates, take the following steps:

1. Call for an appointment. When you call, explain your purpose. In most cases, there will be a charge.
2. Be frank in explaining your resources and hopes and in asking about the lawyer's view on investments, counseling your heirs, and the use of trusts.

   Expertise is important, but you want your widow and children to feel comfortable with the individual you select. Therefore, it's a good idea to bring your spouse along. The meeting will establish a relationship and give the attorney a chance to explain some of the legal requirements involved in planning an estate and what probate is all about.
3. Ask about charges. For estate planning, charges are usually based on time spent. To secure all the facts and properly counsel a client and draft the proper instrument takes time, and time and effort are essentials of the lawyer's product. How often a new client will say, "All I want is a simple will. How much do you charge?" There's a lot more to a responsible job of estate planning than just preparing a will.
4. Look for integrity. By tradition and statute, lawyers have been accorded special privileges and responsibilities. The great majority of them try to maintain high standards, but as in any profession, there are some whose efforts are more geared toward rewarding themselves than serving their clients. Often, such lawyers are good salesmen but poor advisers, especially when confronted with the complexities of estate planning. However, the danger of selecting a lawyer who misrepresents his expertise is lessening as more "victims" file—and win—malpractice suits based on the results of so-called estate planning.

Beware of the lawyer who says that he (or she) will prepare a "simple will" for $25. There is no way a competent job of estate planning and all the counseling that should go into it can be accomplished for such a charge. You may get the $25 will—but that's all you get. Your search for economy may in the end be very expensive.

Drafting a will or trust agreement comes only after thorough analysis, which often results in recommendations for rearranging your holdings to assure a sound, economical long-term program. In other words, it's what happens *before* the preparation of an instrument that takes much of the time.

PROBATE FEES

In the past, state laws set legal fees for the probate of estates on a percentage basis. The fees were the same for easy-to-handle and for relatively complicated estates. Today, enlightened leaders of the legal profession, mindful of the possibility that such fee schedules might restrict competition and anxious to assure charges that are fair to both client and lawyer, recommend charges based upon the work involved, and this normally is on an hourly basis. Figured this way, the fee would then reflect the time involved and the complexity of the estate.

In most cases, probate fees are modest and will not significantly reduce estate assets. They are lowest when the will has been properly drawn and kept up to date, and there has been continuing estate planning. But the charges can escalate when an estate that at first glance appeared routine turns out to involve unreported obligations of the decedent or difficulties develop in administration or disposition of estate assets.

Because of the frequent changes in laws and the spread of special benefits such as retirement plans, the preparation of a will and other estate planning documents is becoming increasingly difficult. That's another reason it pays to start the process early and review one's situation frequently.

Many people are reluctant to accept the cost of estate planning because:

1. Estate planning involves the unpleasant subject of death.
2. In large measure, it relates to something beyond the client's lifetime and to tax savings that will benefit someone else.
3. It is frustrating and, in terms of human nature and usual purchasing habits, uncharacteristic to commit oneself to anything for which there is no sure cost.

Yet lawyers must be compensated for their time and skill. Conceiving and implementing a worthwhile estate plan takes many hours, in which basic data are gathered, alternative recommendations considered, the necessary documents prepared, and the reasons for and terms of the plan explained to the client and his family.

To those unfamiliar with the details of the legal process, the delays that occur in court procedures, and the impact of changes in laws, the fees may seem large. But they represent the time spent—usually months, often years. As pointed out before, in many cases the current fees will be more than offset by future savings.

Few attorneys are able, or find it possible, to set a definite price in advance, especially if they have not had a chance to spend some time with the prospective client and to learn some of the facts of his estate. To expect a lawyer to commit himself on a fee for estate planning is comparable to asking a garage mechanic the cost of repairs before he has examined the damage to the car.

Our experience in the field and our contacts with other estate planners lead us to believe that the best way to handle the problem of proper fees is to have frank discussions on the subject at the beginning of the relationship and regularly over the years. The client has the right to get the lawyer's best estimate of fees and costs for planning and probate.

Our advice: Ask that your attorney set a range within which he expects the charges to fall. In most cases, the final bill will be fairly close to his quotation, but if unusual situations occur or if you change your mind on the disposition of assets, costs will probably be higher.

Once, after due consideration, you have selected your lawyer, you must have confidence that the person you have chosen is an honest, dedicated professional who will do the best job at a reasonable price. After all, legal fees are insignificant if your estate is planned to meet your objectives.

One final point: Do not delay in making a change if, for some reason, you become convinced that you made an error in your choice. Your relationship with your lawyer should be a long-term satisfactory one, and if you feel you have made a mistake, make a change.

REVIEWING ESTATE PLANNING

Estate planning is a never-ending process. Just because you have completed your plan, written a will, and signed various documents, it doesn't mean you can forget your program. Estate plans deal with the future, and so they are subject to change and adjustment.

It is advisable to review your plan every couple of years, preferably with your attorney, and when called for, with other members of your advisory team. Reviewing the plan involves going over the basic documents to see whether they still "fit" or whether changes in your own or your family situation suggest revisions. Every three or four years, you may find it helpful to recalculate your estate and redefine your objectives. This reassessment is especially important if you have inherited money or advanced to a more remunerative position, and if previously dependent young members of the family have become independent or older relatives have become more dependent on you—in short, if there have been any substantial changes in your financial picture.

The purpose of the review is to make certain that your plan is still viable. If it is not, make the necessary adjustments immediately.

One very important time to check your plan is at retirement, when you, and possibly also your spouse, can start getting social security checks or withdrawing benefits from your pension or profit-sharing plan.

Once you have this kind of assured monthly income, you might be in a position to revise your bequests and to start making gifts. All changes should be made within the broad framework of your total estate plan and only after careful consideration of your own needs, of adequate protection for your spouse, and of the financial future of your heirs. Keep in mind that illness in your family may be costly. The money you counted on for a worry-free retirement can be rapidly depleted. And once a gift has been made, there is almost no way to make the beneficiary responsible for proper care of you and your spouse. An experienced lawyer can earn his fee through the counsel he gives at retirement time alone.

9

Choosing trustees and estate administrators

CHOOSING A TRUSTEE

Almost anyone, including the person who establishes the trust (the donor or trustor), can serve as a trustee. It's a fact of life that the one establishing the trust will probably have the greatest interest in and devotion to the trust, but it may not always be practical for him to assume the responsibility. Also, certain tax objectives may not be obtainable if the one establishing the trust also acts as a trustee of it. And of course, there are those most frequent occasions when trusts are established in wills, to become effective after the death of the creator of the will (the testator).

Until recent times, most trustees were individuals, usually relatives or friends, but as the business of property management became more specialized, more trustees have been professionals, typically employees of a bank or trust company. Their fees usually are expressed as a percentage of the assets in the trust. Trust business can be profitable, so there is competition—a fact to remember when you make your choice of a trustee.

Note: When you consider appointing an institution as trustee, be sure the fees are not too high in relation to your trust assets. Most banks have an annual minimum fee of at least $400 and sometimes there are termination fees. Be sure to find out exactly what fees will be charged. When holdings are small, you'll be better off to name a relative or friend.

There are advantages to naming a relative as trustee. For example, you can know that your brother-in-law is familiar with your financial affairs, understands why the trust was created, and has a good relationship with the beneficiaries. Furthermore, he will probably serve for little or no remuneration.

But there are problems with such arrangements:

1. Individuals are mortal. A trustee may die before the end of the trust or become disabled or incapable of handling business matters or making business decisions. It's best to name an alternate trustee at the outset. That way, if for any reason your brother-in-law is unable to act, the alternative person has already been nominated.

An institution, on the other hand, does not become ill or incapacitated and is likely to continue in business. Furthermore, you can get special services such as computer readouts, property management, and portfolio analysis.

2. The interest of an individual trustee may wane if the compensation is not adequate. Whether or not he is a member of the family, a trustee has the right to a fair-value payment for services rendered. The saying "You get what you pay for" is applicable in this situation.

You can get extra services by paying special fees to professionals who can call on their institution's specialized skills and facilities, such as computers. But the individual trustee who performs effectively is well worth the money he requests. He should be paid and the trust instrument should so state.

3. A relative may lack the necessary skills. A relative, though he might be a fine schoolteacher, might not be able to handle a $500,000 trust fund for your widow or heirs. He might simply lack the right experience or temperament for the job.

Many intelligent people have little knowledge of money and property. When a wife and children request funds, the trustee must be able to sort out those needs that are worthwhile and to make allocations in keeping with the intentions of the person who established the trust.

An inexperienced trustee will get on-the-job training at the donor's expense. A few mistakes or inefficient administration can be costly and irritating.

4. The financial responsibility of a relative may not be impeccable. Uncle Joe may be a wonderful fellow, but he may go broke, and then there's no way to get back any money lost through his poor administration. This problem doesn't exist with the corporate fiduciary; it has the resources to pay for possible negligence.

5. A relative may become unavailable because of business or personal commitments. If cousin Bill retires to California, he will not be able to properly supervise a trust in Maine. Or if the trustee has to travel a good deal, he may not be able to spend the time needed to manage the property or to tend promptly to the needs of the beneficiaries.

An institution will not move away and will always have people who are ready to help. The costs to you may be higher, but they are likely to be reasonable because of competition and supervision by the courts.

6. Taxes must be considered. Trusts more often than not are established for tax reasons. The general idea is to give beneficiaries economic benefits from the property held in trust—but in such a way as to not cause the property held in trust to be considered a part of the beneficiary's taxable estate when the beneficiary dies. For this reason, and sometimes for income tax reasons, it is advisable, and sometimes necessary, that one who in no way is a beneficiary be the trustee of the trust.

7. Impartiality is often desirable. Trustees sometimes are called upon to make difficult or unpopular decisions. In divided family situations, often the beneficiaries feel more comfortable if a "neutral" makes the decisions. There are those times when a surviving spouse would like to say "no" to a financial request from a relative; how convenient it is to be able to say, "The bank is handling my affairs; you will have to ask the bank." Usually, that is the last of such requests.

It has been our experience that, as a general rule, an individual trustee is satisfactory for a small trust under $100,000 but an institution is more effective when the assets are greater and involve special management problems or hard-to-please beneficiaries.

CHOOSING AN EXECUTOR

The executor (designated "personal representative" in some states) is the individual or organization responsible for administering your estate. In general, the qualifications needed for executor are similar to those required of a trustee: availability, integrity, administrative ability, financial responsibility, and empathy with the heirs. Executors have great responsibilities. Their duties are called for when you are no longer living—no longer around to "fire" them.

By law, the function of the personal representative is to fulfill the testator's written wishes to complete the steps mandated for an accounting of the disposition of the estate to the beneficiaries, the tax authorities, and the probate court. In the process, he is trying to match the intentions of the deceased with the needs of the heirs and is providing information and peace of mind to the survivors.

Although this sounds like a difficult task, it can usually be done easily enough, unless the estate is huge and diverse. A personal representative needs common sense, the services of a competent lawyer, and a willingness to accept responsibility.

The first step in selecting a personal representative is to ask your attorney about the legal limitations. Some states permit only relatives or state residents to act as executors. In other states, there may be no limitation and you can select any individual or institution, or a combination of both.

Here's a checklist of what to look for in choosing an executor:

Ability to get along with your heirs. This applies primarily to your spouse and children. For most individuals, death is a harsh blow. They need support and solace from a person tactful enough to deal with emotional problems, yet strong enough to get the estate settled quickly and fairly.

To make those difficult and sometimes unpopular decisions, empathy on the part of the executor may be especially important when there's a large family. Younger people and nonblood relatives may be viewed with suspicion and older folks may not be able to get along with nonconforming teen-agers. Ideally, the executor should be able to perceive and minimize the effects of such conflicts.

If you do choose a relative, it's a good idea to decide on someone who is not overly involved in family feuds, has tact and concern, and understands your wishes and your family needs.

Ability to command respect. This is an essential requirement if you anticipate controversy among your heirs or business and professional associates or with governmental agencies. Your spouse may not be the best person to deal with your business associates—particularly when the spouse has only known the business associate on a social basis.

Availability. In settling an estate, there are numerous deadlines, documents that require signatures, and occasions calling for personal involvement of the executor. Postponements due to the absence of the personal representative can be costly to the estate, annoying to your heirs, and inconvenient to the lawyer and the court. Choose someone who is readily available and can get the job done.

Executive and administrative ability. The executor is responsible for providing funds for your family and making the best possible arrangements for the disposition of your estate assets. As in the case of choosing a trustee, what you will need in terms of executive and administrative ability depends a great deal on the type of property you own. If you have considerable real estate or substantial security holdings, look for someone with experience in those specific areas.

But don't place more value on this ability than on the ability to maintain good personal relationships, especially when there are young children involved. Extra money is not as important as understanding for your family.

Finally, in choosing an executor, always consider:

Your spouse. If your spouse has been able to handle you (probably her biggest job), manage the household, and bring up the children, she probably has the ability and common sense to retain competent counsel, make proper judgments, and follow the well-established procedures for settling estates.

Outside aid. Again, as in choosing a trustee, whether or not you select a bank or trust company as the executor depends a good deal on the size and complications of your estate. Financial institutions are experienced, efficient, and skilled in handling taxes, estate planning, and investments. But their officers may be impersonal, their policies arbitrary, and their charges too high to be justified except for estates of more than $200,000.

When you consider a lawyer as executor, find one who is experienced in probate, because such expertise can speed settlement and help keep administrative costs low. Experienced lawyers generally do not like to act as executors. They usually do so only in exceptional situations.

In many cases, the best arrangement may be a combination of a relative and a lawyer or institution as coexecutor. Extablishing dual responsibility may also be a wise solution. For example, an older sister or aunt might be assigned the care of the children and a bank might handle the money. The disadvantages of such an arrangement are that such split responsibility may be awkward and time-consuming, but it can serve a useful purpose if you have qualms about the management skill of the individual you name as executor.

Before you select a professional fiduciary, discuss the fees, philosophy, and method of operation with a representative of the organization. You can change an executor during your lifetime, but once you die, your will is irrevocable and it is difficult to make a replacement.

To summarize: The choice of your trustee and personal representative should be made on the basis of your family's happiness rather than on business or monetary benefits. You are delegating important authority for the administration of your affairs after you are gone!

10

Sample plans

The tables you will find in this chapter provide examples of wise estate planning. Rather than describing the needs of particular individuals, they are meant to point out some ways of solving estate planning problems, based on what age group you belong to, the amount of wealth you have, and your family circumstances. As with medical prescriptions, which should not be taken without the advice of a physician, these plans should not be embarked on except with the counsel of a competent attorney.

For each sample we have proposals that, under current laws, appear to be best suited to the manner in which the assets are held. In everyday life, of course, there will be variations in details.

These samples can only be broad guidelines. They do not take into consideration some of the most essential factors in estate planning: your personal and family objectives, your life style, future inheritances, or decisions relating to the choice of a trustee or executor. As already mentioned several times before, successful implementation of every worthwhile estate plan requires frequent review so changes can be made in line with your greater resources, shifting family situations, and new federal and state laws and regulations. For all these reasons, the sample plans that follow are for illustration, not implementation.

YOUNG MARRIEDS

In our experience, Young Marrieds make up the largest single category of persons in need of estate planning. The typical couples we have in mind have been wed about five years and have one or two children. Their income fluctuates, but because they are so well trained and educated, they can look forward to ever higher earnings. In the early years, when both husband and wife are working, their income is high. However, it drops a bit when the children come and Mrs. Young Married stays home. Then it moves up again when she goes back to work or the husband gets raises or a better position. The point is that this sample plan is a base and should be reviewed and revised frequently.

Although young couples today may seem to have more material possessions than couples in the past, their net estate is still not large. Homes, cars, furniture, and other possessions can be purchased on credit. The down payments they pay are the minimum, especially for homes that can be purchased with minimal cash and a large, long mortgage. In the first years, therefore, the equity of the Young Marrieds may be low, but this is not a good reason for delaying estate planning, especially when there are children.

Usually, the first step Young Marrieds take in estate planning, in order to create an estate rapidly, is to purchase life insurance. Add the group life policies that come with almost every job today, and they then have a total sum of insurance that puts them at a greater level of wealth than that ever attained by their parents—in our sample (Table 3), an estate of $134,000 plus social security.

Note that the two major characteristics of the Young Marrieds' estate are that there is very little probate property and that life insurance is the primary asset. Under the 1976 Federal Tax Reform Law, no federal estate tax is imposed until the adjusted gross estate is over $161,563 in 1980 (and $175,625 or over in 1981 and thereafter). There could, of course, be state taxes, but generally, if there are any, they would usually be insignificant.

The problem that must be provided for is if both parents die. Then there should be some way of caring for the small children and guaranteeing them the full benefits of their parents' combined estates.

The simplest, best solution would be to set up a two-step arrangement:

1. *Have each estate set up so that if one partner dies, the survivor will receive full rights of ownership of the whole estate.* This can be done by having the wife named the primary beneficiary of the husband's personal and group insurance ($100,000) and the husband named the beneficiary of her $10,000 group life policy.

   All other property can be held in joint tenancy. Probably

Table 3 THE YOUNG MARRIEDS

HUSBAND, WIFE AND TWO MINOR CHILDREN; ANNUAL INCOME, $20,000

Life Insurance

Personal Policy (Mr.'s life)	$50,000	
Group Life (Mr.)	50,000	
(Mrs.)	10,000	
		$110,000

Homestead (joint tenancy)

Market Value	$75,000	
Less: Mortgage	(65,000)	
		10,000

Savings and Investments
(joint tenancy)   4,000

Personal Effects	15,000	
Less: Installment Debt	(5,000)	
		10,000

Total   134,000

DISPOSITION OF ESTATE

Husband's Will	*Wife's Will*
1. All my estate to my wife. ⟵————————⟶	1. All my estate to my husband.
2. If my wife does not survive, then estate goes into trust for children.	2. If my husband does not survive, then estate goes into trust for children.
↓	↓
A. Trustee to provide support and education for children.	A. Trustee to provide support and education for children.
B. When youngest child is 21, divide and distribute the estate equally among children.	B. When youngest child is 21, divide and distribute the estate equally among children.

only in such circumstances would we give such blanket advice about dual ownership. When circumstances change—if greater wealth is attained through property acquisition, inheritance, more insurance, or raises—a different method of property ownership should be used.

The fact that household goods are not suitable for holding in joint tenancy presents no problem. Most states have a summary procedure (an abbreviated probate process) to assure transfer of such assets to the surviving spouse.

2. *Establish a trust to take effect only at the death of both parents.* Under this arrangement, all property goes first to the survivor and, at her or his death, to the trust for the benefit of the children. As part of this plan, the contingent beneficiary of all insurance policies should be the trust, so that the children will have the protection they deserve, no matter what happens.

Remember, too, that there are extra benefits due from social security for the widow and children under eighteen (under twenty-two when they are full-time students). The payments will depend on earnings on which social security has been paid and the year of death. When there are two minor children, as in this sample, payments could be in excess of $300 per month per child.

Young Marrieds should make a practice of frequently reviewing their estate plans, because as circumstances change, adjustments will have to be made. In surprisingly few years, the family income may increase and debts be paid off, until the estate will be sizable enough to justify revisions of joint tenancy and, possibly, the establishment of trusts to minimize taxes.

YOUNG EXECUTIVE

The Young Executive who is depicted in this example is already well on his way to financial success. He earns a good income, considerably above the national average for people of his age, and has more of everything: a homestead that is larger and more costly than that of the Young Marrieds (with a bigger mortgage), outside investments, and much more life insurance. His wife is strictly a homemaker and has no separate assets.

The Young Executive puts great emphasis on insurance because of his larger income and because he feels that his family responsibilities are greater than those of the Young Marrieds. In the event of his death, his widow would be under a considerable economic strain in order to maintain her standard of living.

Thanks to the policies of his employer, who is anxious to encourage long-term loyalty, the Young Executive has extra benefits:

1. *A $20,000 vested interest in a retirement plan.* This is the dollar value of the savings set aside, in the profit-sharing plan, to finance the ultimate retirement income. This money will not be fully available until the Young Executive is sixty years old, but the value may be included in his estate if he dies at an earlier age. The amount of federal and state estate taxes, if any, will depend on how the money is paid out at his death. By retirement time, the total will be far greater.

2. *Life insurance of $240,000.* This includes $100,000 personal coverage, $100,000 group insurance, and $50,000 from a specially financed "split-dollar" policy whereby the employer pays that portion of the annual premium that represents the increase in cash value and the employee pays the balance to cover the death benefit cost. Because this arrangement involves borrowing against the cash value of the insurance policy, the net worth, at the time of this sample plan, is $40,000.

   If the Young Executive should die, there would be two beneficiaries: the company would receive the cash value, and the widow (and/or minor children) would get the much greater death benefit.

Example: For a $50,000 "split-dollar" policy, in the first year, the employer would pay nothing toward the cash value and the executive would pay the entire $1,100 premium (possibly borrowed from the company). In the second year, the policy begins to have a cash value, so the company would pay $240 representing the cash value, and the Young Executive $860 and so on. Soon, the individual's contribution would decrease sharply.

Our Young Executive has a wife and three minor children, currently earns $50,000 owns a total of $240,000 in life insurance, and has a vested retirement benefit of $20,000. He owns a $100,000 house with a $60,000 mortgage, has $45,000 in savings and investments, and personal effects valued at $35,000. In the event of his death, his estate would be $380,000.

The Young Executive's sample plan illustrates the use of two aids in estate planning:

1. A pour-over will.
2. A life insurance trust.

Without the $240,000 in life insurance, the Young Executive's estate is not large enough to justify setting up an *inter vivos* trust. In fact, as long as the estate is under about $425,000, there will be no federal tax because of the marital deduction, unified credit, and expenses. But there may be a small death or inheritance tax imposed in some states.

In terms of taxes, the real problem may occur after the death of the survivor, presumably the widow. If the wife does not remarry, on her subsequent death, only about $175,000 will be exempt from federal estate tax. Without proper planning, there would then be substantial taxes to be paid.

Life insurance trust. To deal with such a possibility and also to anticipate greater assets while he is living, the Young Executive should establish a life insurance trust that in the event of the death of the Young Executive would set up two trusts:

1. Trust A, consisting of about $205,000 of his net estate (gross estate less debts and administrative expenses) less any property that the wife receives directly, such as joint tenancy assets. A formula determines the exact amount so that the unified credit and the marital deduction will be used to the best advantage.
2. Trust B, consisting of the remaining assets of the net estate less inheritance taxes, if any.

How the specific assets are divided between the two trusts depends on a number of considerations, including the dictates of federal estate tax regulations and possible future taxes. Generally, however, the allocations will follow the examples described here.

The widow would receive the income from both trusts. She would be able to draw on the principal of Trust A at once, and at her death, could leave the remainder to whomever she named in her will. This provision, called a "general power of appointment," is necessary in order to qualify the estate for the marital deduction. If she does not specify beneficiaries, the balance of the assets of Trust A would pour over into Trust B.

She is entitled to all the income from Trust B after the principal of Trust A has been spent and if she needs extra money to maintain her standard of living or for the education of the children. At her death, the trust would continue for the benefit of the children. The income and principal would be used for their support and education, and at an appropriate time, the estate would be divided and distributed among them. Principal distributions from Trust B during the wife's lifetime and thereafter for the children would be determined by a corporate trustee.

The date and manner of the ultimate allocation of trust assets could vary according to the wishes of the parents. The terms could be written into the original trust, or the trustee might have been given discretionary powers with regard to the allocation.

Some feel that the distribution of assets should be made when the youngest child becomes an adult, at age eighteen, nineteen, or twenty-one, depending on the state of residence. However, our experience has shown that it is better to delay distribution of the principal and, say, give half when each child reaches the age of twenty-five and the balance at thirty.

Employee benefits. Retirement benefits must be handled carefully. Federal estate tax law does not permit a lump-sum distribution to avoid death taxes. It is possible to take the money over a three-year period, but, depending on other factors, such as income taxes, a lump-sum payment may be more advantageous.

An individual who takes early retirement at, say, age sixty-two can take the lump-sum retirement benefit and roll it over into an IRA (Individual Retirement Account). There will be no tax imposed until he withdraws the money.* In the meantime, the executive can take another job, and, in that new position, become a member of another retirement plan with the same tax-deferring benefits. These situations are complex and should be decided upon only after consultation with a tax-knowledgeable lawyer.

The important thing is to stay flexible and consider all the choices. In the sample plan, for instance, the Young Executive would be better

*He must begin to withdraw funds at age seventy and one-half.

off with a lump-sum payment of his retirement benefits at this time. But later, if the value of his retirement fund and his estate grows, another solution might be called for.

Wills. The Young Executive's will is of the "pour-over" type. His life insurance trust is the pillar of his plan. His personal effects pass to his wife and everything else pours over into the life insurance trust, which in turn funnels everything into Trusts A and Trust B by tax-saving formulas.

As we stress throughout this guide, a wife should make a will of her own. Her assets may be small at the outset, but if her husband dies she will be relatively wealthy. Hers should be a simple will that provides that if she dies first, everything goes outright to her husband. If he dies first, all the property she inherits from him, on her subsequent death, will pour over into the life insurance trust. As a result, after the death of both, all assets would be held in trust for the children and there would be no need to appoint a guardian for their estate to handle any assets.

INDEPENDENT BUSINESSMAN

The principal asset in the estate of a small businessman is usually his business. The kind of typical businessman depicted in this sample plan has struggled in the early years, been plagued by a shortage of working capital and frustrated by an inability to borrow sufficient funds for needed expansion and updating of equipment. He does not have access to many corporate benefits and, with his limited resources, has been unable to buy as much life insurance as the Young Executive or to set aside, in a retirement plan, as much as the Professional.

His relatively small amount of insurance is often due to distrust of or skepticism about life insurance, which he feels doesn't provide the opportunity for high percentage growth. Such an attitude is unfortunate because the Independent Businessman needs to protect his family and the value of his business after his death.

The Independent Businessman has a wife and three minor children, earns $60,000 a year, and has assets of $425,000: $100,000 in life insurance; a house with a market value of $100,000 (and a $40,000 mortgage); a business with a net worth of about $200,000; $20,000 in retirement benefits; $10,000 in cash (in his own name); investments of

Table 4 YOUNG EXECUTIVE

WIFE AND THREE MINOR CHILDREN; ANNUAL INCOME, $50,000

Life Insurance		
Personal	$100,000	
Split-dollar	50,000	
Minus: Loan	(10,000)	
Group Life	100,000	
		$240,000
Homestead (joint tenancy)		
Market Value	$100,000	
Less: Mortgage	(60,000)	
		$40,000
Retirement benefits (vested) in Pension, Profit sharing and Stock-option Plans		20,000
Savings and Investments (own name)		45,000
Personal Effects		35,000
Total		$380,000

Table 4 (continued)   D I S P O S I T I O N   O F   E S T A T E

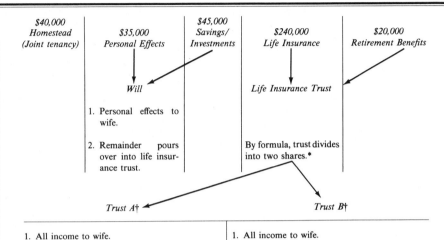

$40,000 Homestead (Joint tenancy)	$35,000 Personal Effects	$45,000 Savings/ Investments	$240,000 Life Insurance	$20,000 Retirement Benefits

Will

1. Personal effects to wife.

2. Remainder pours over into life insurance trust.

Life Insurance Trust

By formula, trust divides into two shares.*

Trust A† ← → *Trust B†*

Trust A†	*Trust B†*
1. All income to wife.	1. All income to wife.

2. Principal to wife at her request.	2. Principal to wife
	   a. After she has used principal in Trust A and
	   b. If she needs it in order to maintain her customary standard of living and for education of children.

3. At wife's death, to whomever she names in will; if she does not name anyone, then to Trust B.	3. At wife's death, trust continues for benefit of children:
	   a. Income and principal to children for their collective support and education.
	   b. When youngest child is 21, trust divided into separate children's shares and, with each share:

Wife's Companion Will	(1) income to each child; (2) principal to each child at trustee's discretion for support and maintenance;
1. All to husband if he survives.	(3) principal distributed
2. If husband doesn't survive, then all to husband's life insurance trust.	½ at age 25 ½ at age 30.

*No reduction is shown as a result of expenses for administration, debts, and costs of last illness. All these expenses would reduce Trust B. Usually, provisions are made for all death taxes to be paid in such a manner as to further reduce Trust B. To proceed otherwise would reduce the marital deduction and, in larger estates, would trigger an increase in federal estate taxes.

†The formula would be flexible to maximize death-tax savings.

$20,000 (securities); and personal effects valued at $15,000.

In planning his estate, he should take two steps:

1. Buy adequate life insurance—about double the $100,000 in the sample. This will allow his widow to receive support while the executor attempts to get a fair price for the business or to hire a manager until a satisfactory sale can be arranged.

   The estate of $425,000 is adequate except that it lacks liquidity at death. There is relatively little cash and insurance in it. As a result, the well-being of this businessman's family depends a good deal on the sale of the business.

   Small businesses are, characteristically, highly personal affairs. The owner is the chief executive, design engineer, personnel officer, planner, public relations director, and salesman. If he dies before the enterprise has established a firm niche in its field and achieved depth in management, the value of the company may be difficult to determine and therefore the proceeds of the sale disappointing. When there is just one key man in a business and he dies, it often is difficult for the executor to capture a sale of the business at a fair price. The buyers all try to purchase it at a bargain price.

2. Groom associates to take over. If the associates show promise, a purchase and sale agreement (also referred to as a "buy and sell") might be considered. For this plan to work, there must be: (a) a seller who has something to sell and is interested in a sale when certain events (such as disability or death) occur; and (b) a buyer (buyers) who is (are) desirous of purchasing at that time.

A purchase and sale agreement brings buyers and sellers together by providing that in the event of the death of one of them, the survivor or survivors will purchase the decedent's interest. Under such an arrangement, there should always be a definite standard of value for the business. Establishing such a financial point of reference (1) provides protection for the family of the deceased because there is a predetermined method of arriving at a purchase price, and (2) allows the new owner(s) freedom to run the company without interference from the decedent's representative, who, probably, will be inexperienced in the field in which the business operates.

The toughest part of such an agreement is setting the selling price.

Formulas are usually inadequate and unsatisfactory. In our experience, it is best to have specific terms, which are mutually agreed upon, reviewed annually, and contain a provision that if the parties fail to agree upon a new value, the old figure will be valid unless it is over two years old. If such terms are not feasible, the agreement should empower a representative of the estate to meet with the purchasers to decide the matter by arbitration if they are unable to agree upon a price.

It is foolish for an Independent Businessman to spend a lifetime building a business and then not be sure of getting adequate value for it in the event of death. That's why we repeat: *For most small enterprises, a purchase and sale agreement is best.*

The money needed to purchase any small business is hard to come by. There is seldom enough cash in the business to do this and outside financing is usually impossible. The most practical method for obtaining the necessary cash is through insurance on the life of the principal owner. This insurance can be purchased by the owner's business associates directly or through the company, and at the owner's death, the proceeds of the insurance will provide sufficient cash for an outright purchase or, at least, a substantial down payment. At a minimum, the insurance should account for about 30 percent of the purchase price of the business, with the balance to be paid in installments plus interest.

THE PROFESSIONAL

This sample plan is designed to characterize the probable situation of a professional such as a physician, a dentist, a lawyer, or an architect —persons with high reoccuring incomes. As a rule, such people operate alone or in small groups, are competent in their fields, but often are removed from the details of business and economics. They need counseling and financial planning advice.

The Professional in our sample is married and has three children: a son in medical school, a married daughter with one infant child, and one youngster still at home. He earns a high income, is able to afford a large home, has several different kinds of investments, and uses life insurance as the major source of his estate building. At the point in his career depicted on Table 6, a life insurance trust would be wise. This would save on estate taxes and protect his family. He needs stable

Table 5 THE INDEPENDENT BUSINESSMAN

WIFE AND THREE MINOR CHILDREN; ANNUAL INCOME, $60,000		
Life Insurance		$100,000
Homestead (joint tenancy)		
Market Value	$100,000	
Less: Mortgage	(40,000)	
Business		$60,000
Book Value	150,000	
Capitalized Earnings* $50,000 × 5	250,000	
	400,000 (divide by 2)	200,000
Retirement Fund		20,000
Cash (own name)		10,000
Investments		
Stocks and bonds		20,000
Personal Effects		15,000
Total		$425,000

*It is often difficult to determine the value of a small business. In many cases, the value shown on the balance sheet (referred to as "book value" and determined by subtracting liabilities from assets) does not reflect its true value. The earning power of the business might be a better indicator. If the business involves little risk, you might multiply the annual earnings by 6 to 10 times to get a fair figure. On the other hand, if a business is relatively small and risky, a multiple of 5 might be more appropriate. This is the process that is known as capitalization of earnings. In this table, the total of bookvalue and earnings capitalized by 5 is divided by 2.

Table 5 (continued) D I S P O S I T I O N O F E S T A T E

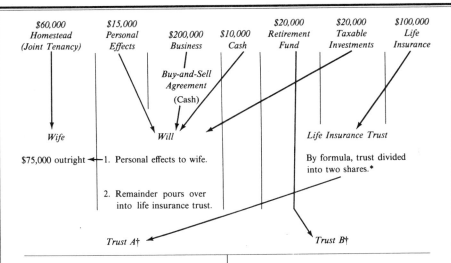

$60,000 Homestead (Joint Tenancy)	$15,000 Personal Effects	$200,000 Business	$10,000 Cash	$20,000 Retirement Fund	$20,000 Taxable Investments	$100,000 Life Insurance

Buy-and-Sell Agreement (Cash)

Wife — $75,000 outright

Will
1. Personal effects to wife.
2. Remainder pours over into life insurance trust.

Life Insurance Trust
By formula, trust divided into two shares.*

Trust A†

1. All income to wife.

2. Principal to wife at her request.

3. At wife's death, it goes to whomever she names in will. If she does not name anyone, then it pours over to Trust B.

Wife's Companion Will

1. All to husband if he survives.

2. If husband doesn't survive, then all to husband's life insurance trust.

Trust B†

1. All income to wife.

2. Principal to wife
   a. after she has used principal in Trust A and
   b. if she needs it in order to maintain her customary standard of living and for education of children.

3. At wife's death, trust continues for benefit of children:
   a. Income and principal to children for their collective support and education.
   b. When youngest child is 21, trust divided into separate children's shares and, with each share:
      (1) Income to each child;
      (2) principal to each child at trustee's discretion for support and maintenance;
      (3) principal distributed
         ½ at age 25
         ½ at age 30.

*No reduction is shown as a result of expenses for administration, debts, and costs of last illness. All these would reduce Trust B. Usually, provisions are made for all death taxes to be paid in such a manner as to further reduce Trust B.

†The formula would be flexible to maximize death-tax savings. In the settlement of the estate, the $250,000 marital deduction would eliminate all, or most, taxes.

assets because, in the past, he has invested in a number of situations, many of which have not fulfilled his expectations.

(Note that a large, ever-increasing portion of his wealth is in his personal retirement plan, which amounts to $50,000 and is growing rapidly as the result of his annual contribution of $7,500 [the normal maximum for a Keogh plan] plus the reinvestment of income and realized appreciation. In another few years, this fund will be worth well over $100,000.)

At this time, the Professional's estate totals $500,000: $200,000 in life insurance, $165,000 in homes (in joint tenancy) and personal effects; $50,000 in a retirement fund; $10,000 cash; investments of $110,000 (in a living trust); and $40,000 worth of assets in his practice. His annual income is $100,000: $95,000 earned and $5,000 from interest and dividends.

Living trust. With such substantial assets, our Professional is ideally situated for setting up a living *(inter vivos)* trust for his investments. As we have seen before, this trust is similar to a life insurance trust except that it is operative during his lifetime.

The usual provisions of such a trust stipulate that the trustor may deposit in, or withdraw from, the trust whenever he pleases. It is the obligation of the trustee to advise him, from time to time, as to the investment of these funds and, during the course of administration, to account for these investments, to produce records, and to provide information about the taxability of the property in the trust.

In the event of the Professional's death, the trust would operate in exactly the same way as the life insurance trust explained earlier. The life insurance can be made payable to this trust in the same manner as if it were a life insurance trust. This procedure will make it possible to avoid the probate process for all assets that are either already in trust or are payable to a trust by way of beneficiary designation other than by will.

If the Professional is in partnership or a member of a professional corporation, there should be a purchase and sale agreement so that the funds tied up in the practice can be obtained quickly after his death.

In the disposition of the Professional's estate, as shown on Table 6, there are two final trusts: Trust A, which takes effect at his death and will total $160,000 after giving effect to the $70,000 (of equity) left outright in the form of the homes held in joint tenancy and the

$20,000 in personal effects (the formula in the living trust will divide the taxable estate in half; Trust A will be $250,000, less the $90,000 outright, or $160,000). If death occurs after 1980 the federal estate tax will be $21,400.

Trust B will receive a total of $250,000. The decision of allocation of assets between Trust A and Trust B is left to the trustee.

Mrs. Professional receives all income of Trust B. She can draw on the principal after she has used the funds in Trust A and if she needs additional money to maintain her customary standard of living and to educate the children. At her death, Trust B is divided into three equal parts. The assets can be distributed to the children or, to provide further protection and tax savings, broken into three separate trusts, each to be administered as follows:

1. Income and principal for support and education.
2. Principal distributed in three payments: one third each time a child reaches the ages of twenty-five, thirty, and thirty-five.

Note that the allocation of trust assets is tailored to the specific needs of the children because of the wide spread in their ages. It would be unwise and possibly unfair to force the oldest child to wait until his youngest brother became an adult. With an estate of this size, early withdrawal of assets will not endanger the economic security of the younger heirs.

Let us emphasize again that Table 6 is only a *suggested* plan. Each family has its own set of circumstances and each estate plan should be drafted to meet the family's distinct needs and wishes. Standardized forms and documents won't do the job.

MR. WEALTHY

The sample plan for Mr. Wealthy is more complex than the previous plans and makes use of several trusts. The trusts are needed, because: (1) Mr. Wealthy's wife has substantial holdings of her own; (2) his parents need financial help; and (3) much of his estate represents the controlling interest in a business corporation.

Mr. Wealthy is worth $4 million, of which $1,900,000 represents control of a closely held corporation. He has a $350,000 mortgage-free home in his own name; $940,000 in investments ($500,000 in real estate, $400,000 in securities, and $40,000 in cash and equivalents);

Table 6 THE PROFESSIONAL.

WIFE AND THREE CHILDREN: SON IN MEDICAL SCHOOL, MARRIED DAUGHTER WITH ONE INFANT CHILD, AND ONE CHILD AT HOME.		
Annual Income	$95,000	
Investment Income	5,000	
Total	$100,000	
Life Insurance		$200,000
Homestead (joint tenancy)		
Market Value	$125,000	
Less: Mortgage	(75,000)	
		50,000
Practice		
Share of equipment	$15,000	
Share of receivables	25,000	
		40,000
Retirement Fund		50,000
Cash		10,000
Investments (own name)		
Saving Certificates	$15,000	
Mutual Fund Shares	20,000	
Stocks and Bonds	50,000	
Real Estate	20,000	
Royalty Interest (oil)	5,000	
		110,000
Vacation Home (joint tenancy)		20,000
Personal Effects		20,000
Total		$500,000

Table 6 (continued)   D I S P O S I T I O N   O F   E S T A T E

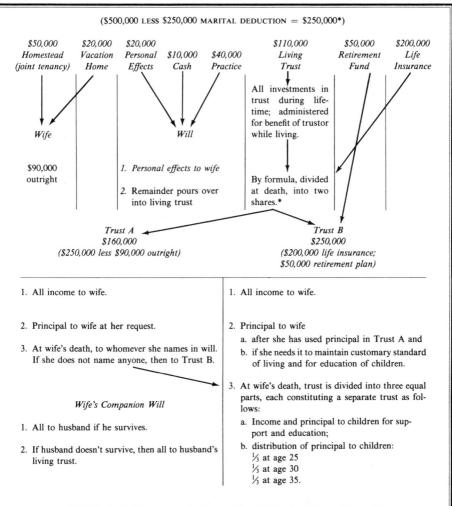

($500,000 LESS $250,000 MARITAL DEDUCTION = $250,000*)

| $50,000 Homestead (joint tenancy) | $20,000 Vacation Home | $20,000 Personal Effects | $10,000 Cash | $40,000 Practice | $110,000 Living Trust | $50,000 Retirement Fund | $200,000 Life Insurance |

Wife

Will

All investments in trust during life-time; administered for benefit of trustor while living.

$90,000 outright

1. *Personal effects to wife*

2. Remainder pours over into living trust

By formula, divided at death, into two shares.*

Trust A
$160,000
($250,000 less $90,000 outright)

Trust B
$250,000
($200,000 life insurance; $50,000 retirement plan)

1. All income to wife.

2. Principal to wife at her request.

3. At wife's death, to whomever she names in will. If she does not name anyone, then to Trust B.

Wife's Companion Will

1. All to husband if he survives.

2. If husband doesn't survive, then all to husband's living trust.

---

1. All income to wife.

2. Principal to wife
   a. after she has used principal in Trust A and
   b. if she needs it to maintain customary standard of living and for education of children.

3. At wife's death, trust is divided into three equal parts, each constituting a separate trust as follows:
   a. Income and principal to children for support and education;
   b. distribution of principal to children:
      ⅓ at age 25
      ⅓ at age 30
      ⅓ at age 35.

*No reduction is shown as a result of expenses for administration, debts, and costs of last illness. All these would reduce Trust B. Usually, provisions are made for all death taxes to be paid in such a manner as to further reduce Trust B.

$300,000 in life insurance; $340,000 in a retirement trust; and $170,-000 representing a vacation home, interest in a hunting lodge, country club memberships, and personal effects, including gun and art collections.

Mrs. Wealthy has $295,000 in her own name: $200,000 in inherited securities and $95,000 in jewelry, furs, silver, and other possessions.

Mr. Wealthy's income is $280,000: $150,000 in salary and $130,000 from investments. In addition, his wife gets $12,000 a year from her stocks and bonds. Together, they pay a proportionately high percentage of their income in federal and state income taxes.

The Wealthys have their house in the husband's name in order to avoid the kind of potential problems regarding joint tenancy mentioned in Chapter 4. With their substantial assets, the Wealthys might be subject to questions, by IRS and state tax authorities, as to the source of funds used to buy property, to make other investments, and so on.

Mr. Wealthy's personal effects are considerable, so he should make preliminary arrangements for their distribution. He could allocate items with sentimental value in an informal letter or memorandum attached to his will, but larger assets, such as the collections, should be subject to specific instructions to the executor in his last testament. That's one of the important duties of a personal representative.

Mr. Wealthy's estate plan should make use of trusts in order to avoid or minimize taxes, to retain control of the business, and to be certain that the disposition of the estate will be handled by knowledgeable professionals.

For example, he might use a short-term (Clifford) trust to aid his parents. This would last for their lifetimes or ten years, whichever is shorter. From his ample investments, Mr. Wealthy can afford to divert taxable income to provide financial assistance and economic security for his mother and father. Such an arrangement will reduce the income taxes of the Wealthys, and if his parents do have to pay taxes on their income, the levies will be small.

Mr. Wealthy is careful about what goes into the trust because he knows that he must give up some measure of control of the assets thus diverted until the death of both parents or until after ten years have passed. He would not want to include any of his business stock, because his lack of control over the property, while it was in the trust, might seriously hamper his administration of the business.

He should consider real estate for insertion in the short-term trust because the management of his real estate, through an agent, would not demand his personal attention or talents. The best property for such a trust would be an income-producing building that has been owned for some time so that its depreciation is no longer much of a factor in reducing Mr. Wealthy's personal income tax liabilities.

Because Mr. Wealthy has a considerable number of other assets, and because most of his workday is taken up in the running of his business, he, like Mr. Professional, should take advantage of a living trust (further discussed hereafter).

Before explaining how Mr. Wealthy uses his trusts, let's see whether or not he can benefit from gifts. Until the 1976 Federal Tax Reform Act, wealthy people could reduce death taxes by making lifetime gifts to children and grandchildren. Often, these gifts were made through trusts because the recipients were not considered mature enough to deal with the property at the time of transfer.

The old pre-1976 law allowed each giver a $3,000 annual exemption per individual recipient and a $30,000 lifetime exemption, and it set gift tax rates at two thirds to three quarters of death tax rates.

But now that there's a unified system, under which gift and death tax rates are the same, and there is no lifetime exemption, there is little advantage to be gained in making substantial gifts. Only two possible avenues for tax reduction remain:

1. The $3,000-per-year-per-individual exemption is still available, but if made to a minor, it must come under his control when he becomes of legal age. Longer-term trusts, for example, won't work.
2. Gifts that are over $3,000 a year may still be worthwhile when the donated property is likely to appreciate in value. The recipient of the gift (donee) gets the giver's (donor's) tax basis. When a gift other than cash is eventually sold, there will be a capital gains tax on all appreciation since the donor's time of purchase.

Thus, the Wealthys' opportunities for saving taxes by making gifts have been seriously limited under the new law.

Since Mr. Wealthy's business represents a substantial portion of his total estate, and since he has every intention of treating his children equally with regard to the distribution of his estate, he faces an estate planning problem if he wants to assure, as he does, that his oldest son acquires ultimate control of the business. Yet he also wants to make sure that his other children receive an equal share of his estate. One of the solutions available to him is to reorganize or recapitalize his business to produce two kinds of stocks: nonvoting preferred and voting common stocks. The voting common stock will be needed by his son for control of the business. The preferred, which does not enjoy a vote but represents value and will usually pay regular dividends, can be used to equalize the inheritance by passing to the other children.

In making these gifts, Mr. Wealthy will have to recognize the new limitations placed upon lifetime transfers by the unified rate system, as explained above.

Other trusts might include:

1. *An irrevocable life insurance trust* which would care for Mrs. Wealthy and eventually be divided among his heirs could save death taxes at both his and his spouse's deaths.

   The disadvantage in having such a trust is that Mr. Wealthy would lose control of the insurance, which might be useful for collateral in an emergency.

2. *Living trust.* A portion of his investments could be placed in an inter vivos trust. During his lifetime it would be administered, and the income distributed, according to his directions. He would receive income and principal as he requested or needed it. After his death, for example, the assets would be divided into Trusts A and B, all income from Trust A to go to his widow, with principal to be used at her request, and, at her death, to go to whomever she names in her will. If she preferred not to name beneficiaries, the assets of Trust A remaining at her death would go into Trust B.

   Trust B would consist of the assets remaining after one half of his net estate assets had gone outright to his wife or to Trust A and after death taxes and administration expenses. With Trust B, the income might be divided ("sprinkled") among his wife and children according to their relative needs and tax circumstances. Principal could be used for the care and maintenance of Mrs. Wealthy after she has exhausted the liquid principal of Trust A. Principal could also be distributed among children if they needed it, as determined by a corporate trustee. Mrs. Wealthy would also have the power at her death, to allocate Trust B among the children and grandchildren, outright or in continuing trusts. This is referred to as "limited" or "special power of appointment." If Mrs. Wealthy fails to exercise this power, Trust B would continue after Mrs. Wealthy died, as shown on Table 7.

Mrs. Wealthy. If Mrs. Wealthy, who has an estate of her own, dies first, there is little need for her to pass her property on to her husband. He has sufficient wealth and the inheritance would only mean added taxes when he dies. For this reason, it might be wise for Mrs. Wealthy to provide that her estate bypass her husband in favor of her children and grandchildren—or be used in some other way.

If Mr. Wealthy's financial situation were such that he felt he might need his wife's assets, should she predecease him, then her will could leave her assets to him. Mr. Wealthy could defer a final decision on taking the assets until his wife's death. If he had no need of them, he would disclaim all or part of them and they could go to the children. In the model depicted in Table 7, we assume that this situation will not occur.

For an alternative way to make sure that her husband is never without funds, Mrs. Wealthy could leave her entire estate in a trust that made her husband and the children "sprinkle beneficiaries" of income and principal at the discretion of a disinterested third-party trustee. Mr. Wealthy would never own or control the principal of the trust, so its assets would not be considered part of his taxable estate at his death.

If Mr. Wealthy died first, Mrs. Wealthy could also consider:

1. *Leaving everything directly to her children:* She and her husband having worked together in planning their estates, and the distributive portions of Mr. Wealthy's living trust being agreeable to her, Mrs. Wealthy need not go into great detail in her trust document. She could provide that all or part of her assets, at death, pour over into her husband's trust and be allocated according to its terms and conditions.
2. *Leaving all or part of her estate to a trust for the benefit of the grandchildren:* The income and principal would be used for

their support and education and the assets divided as each reached maturity, or partially allocated at designated ages.

The Wealthys should consider charities. Gifts to charity can be made directly or retained in trust and parceled out periodically as the trustee sees fit. The easiest and least expensive method is to make outright gifts to charities. But if the Wealthys have a special cause they are interested in, or want to retain greater control over the distributions, they may create a charitable foundation or trust. The foundation can be created during their lifetime or through their wills or trusts. Foundations are for the wealthy. They require considerable thought and professional advice.

As might be expected, the Wealthy family estate plan is much more detailed and diverse than the previous plans (see Table 7). The Wealthys obviously can afford to expend much time and effort on estate planning.

Table 7 MR. WEALTHY

Family

Son	(33) married, 2 children. Employed in the family business. Father would like to have him run it some day.
Son	(31) married, 2 children. Established physician.
Daughter	(26) married, 1 child. Husband employed by large corporation and family subject to frequent moves.
Son	(17) doesn't know what he wants to do, but leans toward art or other activity allowing him to work with his hands.

Husband's parents are comfortable, but their resources have been depleted by illness.

MR. WEALTHY'S PRESENT ESTATE

Life Insurance		$300,000
Homestead (own name)		
Market Value	$350,000	
Less: Mortgage (none)	0	
		350,000
Investments (own name)		
Stock Portfolio	$300,000	
Municipal Bonds	100,000	
Real Estate (apartment houses)	400,000	
Real Estate (unimproved)	100,000	
Cash and Equivalents	40,000	
		940,000
Retirement Fund		340,000
Business Interest (own name, controlling interest in closely held corporation)		1,900,000
Vacation Home (own name)		30,000
Hunting Lodge Interest, Country Club Memberships		25,000
Personal Effects		
Household furnishings and automobiles	$50,000	
Gun collection	15,000	
Art collection	50,000	115,000
Total		$4,000,000

Table 7 (continued)   D I S P O S I T I O N   O F   M R.   W E A L T H Y 'S   E S T A T E

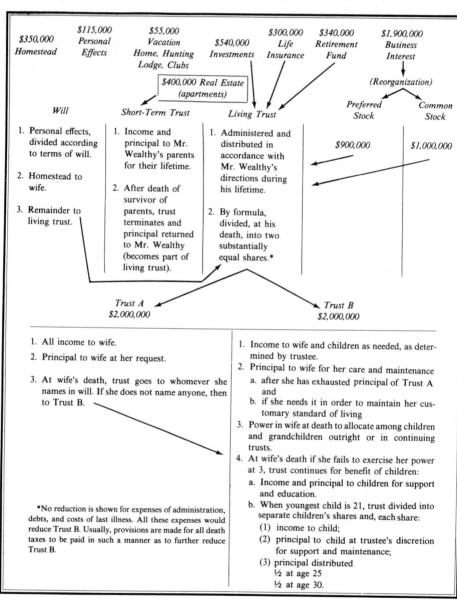

| $350,000 Homestead | $115,000 Personal Effects | $55,000 Vacation Home, Hunting Lodge, Clubs | $540,000 Investments | $300,000 Life Insurance | $340,000 Retirement Fund | $1,900,000 Business Interest |

$400,000 Real Estate (apartments)

(Reorganization)

| Will | Short-Term Trust | Living Trust | Preferred Stock | Common Stock |

Will

1. Personal effects, divided according to terms of will.

2. Homestead to wife.

3. Remainder to living trust.

Short-Term Trust

1. Income and principal to Mr. Wealthy's parents for their lifetime.

2. After death of survivor of parents, trust terminates and principal returned to Mr. Wealthy (becomes part of living trust).

Living Trust

1. Administered and distributed in accordance with Mr. Wealthy's directions during his lifetime.

2. By formula, divided, at his death, into two substantially equal shares.*

$900,000 $1,000,000

Trust A $2,000,000

Trust B $2,000,000

1. All income to wife.

2. Principal to wife at her request.

3. At wife's death, trust goes to whomever she names in will. If she does not name anyone, then to Trust B.

*No reduction is shown for expenses of administration, debts, and costs of last illness. All these expenses would reduce Trust B. Usually, provisions are made for all death taxes to be paid in such a manner as to further reduce Trust B.

1. Income to wife and children as needed, as determined by trustee.

2. Principal to wife for her care and maintenance
   a. after she has exhausted principal of Trust A and
   b. if she needs it in order to maintain her customary standard of living

3. Power in wife at death to allocate among children and grandchildren outright or in continuing trusts.

4. At wife's death if she fails to exercise her power at 3, trust continues for benefit of children:
   a. Income and principal to children for support and education.
   b. When youngest child is 21, trust divided into separate children's shares and, each share:
      (1) income to child;
      (2) principal to child at trustee's discretion for support and maintenance;
      (3) principal distributed
          ½ at age 25
          ½ at age 30.

Table 7 (continued)   D I S P O S I T I O N   O F   M R S.   W E A L T H Y 'S   E S T A T E

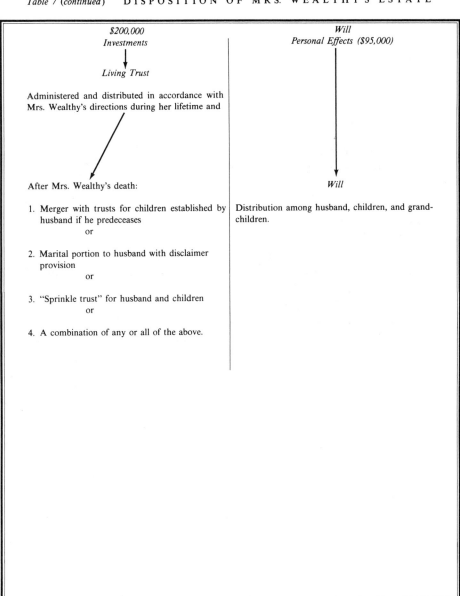

$200,000
Investments

↓

Living Trust

Administered and distributed in accordance with
Mrs. Wealthy's directions during her lifetime and

After Mrs. Wealthy's death:

1. Merger with trusts for children established by
   husband if he predeceases
                 or

2. Marital portion to husband with disclaimer
   provision
                 or

3. "Sprinkle trust" for husband and children
                 or

4. A combination of any or all of the above.

Will
Personal Effects ($95,000)

↓

Will

Distribution among husband, children, and grandchildren.

In conclusion

Now you know that there are a number of things you ought to understand in planning your estate. Some of our suggestions and the advice given through the samples will save you money and taxes; other ideas can provide greater security for your loved ones. Taken together, they point the way to a more financially rewarding career while you live and protection for your heirs after you die.

We hope that after reading this guide, you will realize that the single most important action you can take to achieve a useful estate plan is to choose a competent lawyer, and when necessary, other knowledgeable, concerned advisers. Estate planning is too complex and ever-changing to be a do-it-yourself project. One mistake will cost you more, in dollars, inconvenience, and suffering, than the fee for the finest attorney.

Glossary

The following are broad definitions of the words to be found most frequently in trust agreements and wills. Your lawyer can explain the terms in greater detail as the occasion requires.

Assets: What the estate owns: cash, savings accounts, insurance, real estate, stocks and bonds, jewelry, automobiles, furniture, rights to pension plan proceeds, and so on.

Beneficiary: The person designated to receive the income and/or principal of a trust or an estate.

Codicil: An amendment to a will.

Corpus: The principal of a fund or an estate, as distinct from interest or income thereon.

Donee: A person to whom a gift is made.

Donor: A person who makes a gift (also called grantor, settlor, trustor).

Estate Planning: The process of planning for the administration and ultimate distribution of one's property. Although usually involving deceased person's property, estate planning can involve the administration of property for a living owner.

Executor: A person or institution named in a will to carry out the instructions of the will. Same as Personal Representative.

Grantor: See Donor.

Intestate: To die without a will.

Irrevocable: An arrangement which *cannot* be changed.

Joint-Tenancy: A form of shared ownership where two or more persons own equal interests in certain property and where the surviving joint-tenant or joint-tenants receive title to the property automatically without need for probate.

109

Life Estate: The right to the use of or income from property during one's lifetime.

Life Tenant: A person holding a life estate.

Non-Probate Estate: Property of a deceased person which passes to beneficiaries or persons sharing ownership in the property which is not subject to the probate process.

Personal Representative: Same as Executor.

Principal: See Corpus.

Probate: A legal process for determining the instructions of a deceased person regarding his property and seeing that they are carried out.

Probate Estate: Property of a deceased person which is subject to probate.

Remainder: The right to property following the death of a life tenant.

Residue: What is left of an estate after specific gifts, administrative expenses, fees and (usually) taxes.

Revocable: An arrangement, such as a trust, which can be changed.

Settlor: See Donor.

Tenancy in Common: A form of shared ownership where two or more persons own equal interests in certain property and where the interest of the deceased tenant is subject to probate.

Testate: A person who dies with a will. (Intestate = without a will.)

Testator: A person who makes a will.

Trust: A legal entity which is created by the owner of property for the purpose of administering and distributing such property for the benefit of the owner and/or other persons.

Trustee: The individual or organization charged with the management and administration of the assets assigned to a trust.

Trust Fund: A fund, established by trust, for the benefit of an individual or organization.

Trustor: See Donor.

Index